HOW *NOT* TO MAKE IT

IN HOLLYWOOD

HOW *NOT* TO MAKE IT

IN HOLLYWOOD

BUT HAVE A HELAVA GOOD TIME TRYING

Brendan Shepherd

and

Sarah Reid

Roads Press

Disclaimer: Some names have been changed to protect the not so innocent. You know who you are.

Printed in the United States of America

Acknowledgements, Dedications and Thanks to Rabbis, Lawyers and Priests everywhere. Without them in your pocket, no one would make it in Hollywood.

Clearly, we had none of the above; however, we did have support from great friends and family.

CONTENTS

Prologue

DUMB AND DUMBER. 1994.

Directed by the Farrelly Brothers.

Starring Jim Carrey and Jeff Daniels.

Tagline: "What the one doesn't have, the other is missing."

This is a story of our experiences on the quest to be Hollywood film producers. It's a handbook as well. You can pay attention to the lessons we've learned and try not to follow our mistakes, or you can do it your way. Do we have regrets? You betcha. But we wouldn't have traded one minute of the madness. There's only a small percentage of people who have gone where we've been, and there's a huge percentage who ache to go, but never will.

INT. RECEPTION OFFICE. HERIGATE FINANCIAL - GLENDALE, CA. - AFTERNOON

Two women, BRENDAN and SARAH enter a dimly lit office.

There is a framed sign above the door that reads, *We Aim to*

Please. A big-haired SECRETARY sits at a large metal desk

staring at her computer. Brendan and Sarah introduce

themselves. The Secretary looks at the two women up and

down and gives them a phony forced smile.

Sarah extends her hand to the Secretary.

SARAH

Hi, we have an appointment.

The Secretary ignores Sarah's handshake, going for her coffee

cup instead.

SECRETARY

Have a seat.

They sit. The Secretary returns her attention to her computer's

monitor. Her frozen stare on the monitor seems eerie to the

two women – like she's having some quiet kind of seizure.

There is a small amount of spittle in the corner of her mouth.

After a few moments, Sarah breaks the uncomfortable silence.

SARAH

You sound like you have an accent. Where are you from?

This jolts the secretary from her trance. She nervously starts

arranging the many pictures on her desk, wipes the corner of

her red lips with her redder fingernails, then begins typing on

her keyboard.

SECRETARY

I'm from Georgia.

Brendan speaks up in a perky voice.

BRENDAN

I grew up in West Virginia

SARAH

I'm from Texas. Born and raised.

The secretary, raising one of her over plucked eyebrows, looks

at the two women.

SECRETARY

Uh, Huh.

She gets up from her desk, picks up her lipstick-stained coffee

mug and walks out of the office and down the hall. Sarah and

Brendan lean over in their seats and watch her go around a

corner. Suddenly, DAN, THE FINANCE MAN's door flies

open and out walks two men - one dressed in plaid shorts and a

chartreuse polo shirt and another totally in black who looks like a sleazy porn director. The two men shake hands. The PORN DIRECTOR's nails are dirty. Brendan and Sarah shoot upright in their seats as though they were marionettes and someone pulled their strings.

PORN DIRECTOR (To Dan, The Finance Man)

I'd like to have the deal done by next month.

Dan, the Finance Man smiles a crooked smile with bonded teeth that look too big for his mouth, and pats the Porn Director on the back.

DAN, THE FINANCE MAN

No problem. We'll call you next week.

He turns to Sarah and Brendan. Another overly big smile crosses his face. He looks the two women up and down, just as the secretary had done. Both women jump to their feet as if avoiding a snake that has slithered under their chair. Without

any introductions, the two women are invited into Dan's office.

DAN, THE FINANCE MAN

Hi, gals. Come on in.

Brendan and Sarah cautiously enter his cluttered office and

take a quick glance around the room. There are pictures on

every wall, covering very old 70's wallpaper and dirty brown

shag carpeting on the floor. Mostly, the pictures are of race

cars and drivers. Brendan and Sarah don't recognize anyone -

or the names of the black permanent marker signatures written

across the pictures, which all look like the same handwriting.

In some of the pictures, it appears as though Dan's image has

been cut and pasted on. After brief introductions and a minor

uncomfortable pause, Sarah speaks.

SARAH

We understand that you have money for film production.

That's what we're here for.

Dan laughs like a joke has been told. Too much and too hard

laughter.

DAN, THE FINANCE MAN

We can get money for anyone for anything. That's what I do.

And I'm good at it. How much are you looking for?

SARAH

We have a script with a budget of three to five million.

He tugs at some paperwork in his desk drawer. It's stuffed full

of papers and they explode out of the drawer. Sarah and

Brendan help him pick them up. He is non-phased by the

interruption. He passes over a couple of crumpled legal sized papers to the two women.

DAN, THE FINANCE MAN

Now if you both would fill out these credit applications and send them back to us as soon as possible with $75.00, we can get started on getting you money for your film.

BRENDAN

Don't you want to hear what we have first?

DAN, THE FINANCE MAN

Oh, sure. Anything with John Travolta attached?

SARAH

Why do you need to do a credit check?

DAN, THE FINANCE MAN

Well, I need to be comfortable knowing who it is

I'm working with. We're talking about giving you a lot of

money. I want to be sure you're not in any trouble.

$75.00 is not much for that kind of research. Is it?

The two women look at each other for reassurance.

BRENDAN

Is that $75.00 for the two of us?

DAN, THE FINANCE MAN.

No. Come on now. It's $75.00 each.

Sarah and Brendan look at each other again. They turn back to

Dan.

SARAH

How long before we know if we are

qualified to get the money?

DAN, THE FINANCE MAN

As soon as we get the $75, we will get right on it. As a matter

of fact, can you write a check today? That way, by next week

we'll have an answer for you.

Dan's eyes light up as though he's solved the problem to global

warming.

DAN, THE FINANCE MAN

Yeah, that's a great idea. You give me a check

today. Then my secretary will call you

next week. We'll definitely know by then.

The women pull out two checks from their file folder and begin writing –

Seventy five dollars and no sense.

The end.

Or, rather, the beginning of the end…

1

WORKING GIRL. 1998.

Directed by Mike Nichols.

Starring Harrison Ford and Melanie Griffith.

Tagline: "For anyone who's ever won. Or anyone who's ever lost.

And for everyone who's still in there trying."

BRENDAN

This was the first of many lessons we learned about making movies - one of the least expensive lessons. We filled out the paperwork and gave him the money and waited for exactly one week to call back. We left pleasant voice messages the first two times we called. After the second week came and went, we left a message with the bored secretary for her boss to give us a call - immediately. He didn't call that week, or the next, or the one after that. We called every few days to see if we could find out what the status was on "our money." Of course, both of our $75 checks were cashed and the credit reports were never done - discovering that much later. We were confused. We were confident that our credit was impeccable so we couldn't understand what the problem was.

The problem was that in all of our extensive production experience, Sarah and I never had to raise money, and we didn't know how.

This quest to produce our own films began a few months before this incident...

I was working for the Walt Disney Company at Buena Vista Home Entertainment, developing and programming children's product. My department mostly developed and produced Disney's sing-along videos; but it was getting smaller by the day – downsizing - and I was anxious to move on - and be creative again. Also, I was getting a little disenchanted with the politics of this huge and haughty corporation.

About six months previously, our vice president, Eleanor Richman became ill and had to take a leave of absence. When she returned a month before her contract was to expire, (still not fully recovered, but fearing for her job) she discovered that they were not going to renew it, and in fact, she told me that they planned to get rid of her. El and I had become friends, and she confided some of what she was going through with me. Those "friends" of hers in high places at Disney turned their backs to her dilemma. She was on her own, fighting the battle to keep her job as well as her life. She told me that only after she threatened to go to the press did she get some results. It certainly wouldn't have looked good if Disney got rid of an employee of ten years who had cancer and wouldn't be able to get decent affordable health insurance. She remained in her position, but she told me that her salary was cut as well as the

perks she previously had enjoyed. I was happy to see that
Disney had a heart.

At Disney we were making the half-hour live action sing-
alongs for around $700,000 to $800,000. In the past, I had
worked on feature projects that were made for much less – like
$500,000 less. And some of them weren't so bad. I learned
how to be creative with a little money. I figure if you learn
how to make movies for $200,000, then when you get $10
million, there's no excuse for not making a good film. But in
reality, there are a hundred million dollar budgeted films that
are lousy.

Before Disney, I had a lot of free lance film experience –
mostly on low budget independent films. During this time is
when I met Sarah. We worked together on a Miramax film,
Roadflower. We never made it to the end of the film, but had a
great time on location in Las Vegas for two months before the

production temporarily closed down. They started up again, I went back to Las Vegas (This time without Sarah) and ended up being stabbed in the back by an overly ambitious assistant.

Note: BE AWARE OF WOLVES IN SHEEP CLOTHING

SARAH

I had worked in the film business for fifteen years. Mostly, I production-managed and coordinated commercials as well as some feature films. I had just gone through an unpleasant divorce and took off for Italy for a few months. When I returned to LA, I took a photography class and tried to focus on what I wanted to do next. I just didn't know. I had already decided that the only way to work in the film business was to do my own thing, but I wasn't even sure that I wanted to do that. Brendan and I had worked together on a few projects, so when she called to ask me if I would be interested in starting a production company with her, I said, "Yes, only if we can do it our way."

BRENDAN

I remember it as Sarah calling *me* to see if *I* wanted to start a production company with *her*. I thought, "Why, not?" We were always quite a team. Both of us were pretty gutsy – an asset in the film business. The prospect of having my own company was exciting and change always suits my nomadic spirit. I was more than ready to move on to something new.

Sarah and I loved the idea of creating our own business; but we weren't exactly sure what to do next - after our decision to be producers. The most logical thing was to find a name for our new company. Sitting over cocktails at Pinot Bistro and coffee at Starbucks, we endeavored to find a perfect name. After coming up with more than twenty possibilities, we came up with "Amazon Films." Our decision was based upon a few things: We wanted to be in the first alphabetical section of anything to do in the film business, it had strong women recognition and Amazon.com was the hot new Internet company. And we did consider ourselves warriors. Once we decided upon the name, we went to the Art Department at Santa Monica Community College and put up a flyer asking for someone to create a logo for us. I think we paid the graphic art student twenty-five dollars for the design. And an extra forty dollars for re-works.

Our goal was to produce our first film for around three to five million dollars. Sarah had a neighbor in Marina del Rey, Matt B, who had raised large sums of money for real estate deals. He was this average-looking older man who seemed thrilled to be around movie people and told us that he always wanted to be in the entertainment business. Matt said that he had numerous contacts in banking and finance and assured us that he could get us money for a film. We believed that he could. There was no reason not to – he said he could.

He bragged that he had just raised over $15 million on a real estate deal. He said that he had good connections with Wells Fargo. We thought, "Yeah, that's a big bank." When those connections didn't come through, he told us that he would set up meetings in Switzerland for us with Credit Suisse. "Yeah, we've heard about Credit Suisse. They're big too." As the weeks rolled by, we kept him informed of our daily accomplishments and finally pressed him for a date of the meeting – we needed to make flight arrangements. After a month of vague reasons why it was difficult (and high priced lunches at The Ivy, which *we* paid for) he finally confessed that none of his contacts wanted to put money into the film business.

Note: WOULD AND COULD ARE DIFFERENT

2

MONEY PIT. 1986.

Directed by Richard Benjamin.

Starring Tom Hanks and Shelley Long.

Tagline: "Deeply in love or deeply in debt?"

BRENDAN

The American Film Market (AFM) was about to begin in a
couple of weeks in Santa Monica, so Sarah and I did some
brain storming about how we were going to participate. This is
the annual LA event where distributors come from all over the
world to buy and sell films. Mostly there are B movies being
distributed at AFM. Lot's of low budget action films with
plenty of "T & A" - and Horror films too.

We came up with an idea to create our own market and
unofficially called it OTM (The Other Film Market).

We put ads in the *Hollywood Reporter* and *Variety* seeking finished films to sell to distribution companies and scripts to develop. We found five fairly good films. A couple of dramas and a couple of comedies - and one that really didn't fit into a specific category. We had several completed short films, but we didn't know exactly what to do with them.

Finally, we had a few good scripts. One that we both liked was *The Martini,* an action comedy about two college students crossing paths with the Mafia.

Before the AFM market began, Sarah and I did some strategizing. We had to create a little publicity for ourselves, so we devised our plan. To get distributors to look at our films, we had to figure out a way to get them to our office. We decided it would be perfect to host a cigar and champagne cocktail hour which would hopefully entice both men and

women from the distribution companies to our office. Office?
What office?

Loews Hotel in Santa Monica, where the American Film
Market was taking place, had no vender rooms left to rent –
and at $9000 per room for the ten day period, that was way out
of our league - so we scouted around for someplace else. After
a lot of knocking on doors, we finally found our office.

The Ocean Lodge was a small hotel just across the street from
the official event at Loews. We took the upstairs room facing

the street - and Loews. We placed a huge canvas banner across the entire top of the hotel with our company's name and new logo in purple print - Amazon Films. We were on a shoestring budget, so we bought stylish furniture from Pier One Imports and two weeks later returned it. I looked up "ethics" on Wikipedia and "film entertainment" wasn't mentioned.

Now that we had our office, we could move forward. The first thing we did before the market began was create our own Amazon Films postcard to be used as an invitation. Since we couldn't afford a graphic designer nor a photographer, we did it all ourselves. A week before AFM, Sarah came over to my place at Studio City with her camera and new knowledge of photography. We drove around looking for a "beautiful woman" who would be the cover girl on our postcard. LA is the capital of stunning women sitting at outdoor coffee shops sipping fat free lattes. Mostly, they are aspiring actresses.

We cruised Ventura Blvd. looking for our cover girl. This day was no different. There were plenty to choose from. At a small outdoor café in Studio City sat a gorgeous blonde about twenty years old sipping her decaf latte. Sarah pulled up to the curb and I ran over to the woman. "How'd you like to be on a postcard?" "Sure," she quickly replied, without asking much more. I explained to her what we were doing, and Sarah got out her camera. We put her in a red dress of Sarah's and set her up with props - a martini glass and a cigar . She looked great.

We had cleared the impromptu shoot with the owner of the café, but it took longer to do than we thought, and the owner was getting a little pissy. I'm not sure of what; if anything, more people were stopping at the café to see what was going on. In Hollywood, everyone wants to be a star. And by hanging out, just perhaps they may get discovered at a coffee shop. It's cliché, but true.

We got the shot we were looking for after lots of shooting. The woman photographed well when she wasn't smiling. She had very bad teeth. Since she had some kind of Eastern European accent, we figured that a lack of fluoride was her demise. But the smirk worked. We took the photo to a place in Hollywood who specializes in postcards and in a few days we had them.

AMAZON

● Features ● Shorts ● Screenplays
OFM
(The Other Film Market)
across from Lowes Hotel
10AM - 5PM

Join us for
Champagne & Cigars
3-5PM

520 Washington Blvd., Suite 475
Marina Del Rey, CA 90292

Next, we bought cigars. I created our own bands from my computer. Sarah and I sat on my living room floor for two days banding them with "Amazon Films." My fingers smelled for a week, but the cigars looked good. We also learned that a good place to store cigars is in the bottom shelf drawer of a refrigerator with a piece of lettuce to keep them moist. Just don't put carrots or onions in with them - everything will smell of cigars and the cigars will have a funky aroma.

We then bought 10 cases of an Australian sparkling wine which we passed off as champagne. Actually, it wasn't too bad for $4.95 a bottle. We planned to have happy hour at our office everyday from three to five pm.

Most of the films that we represented had some kind of finished artwork. Several had posters that we hung on the walls. I brought my Persian rug from home to cover the grungy carpet and we had fresh flowers on a table everyday, thanks to Sarah's roses from her garden. The mediocre little room looked pretty good.

There were two other production companies in the hotel and they were enthusiastic about being part of our PR ingenuity.

One company in the suite below us had a script with a fairly decent cast attached to it. At first, the producer of the film was friendly and came to our office everyday. We noticed that an old lady would arrive in her white Jag around noon each day to visit the producer. After about five minutes, they would argue. It was truly like a scene from *Sunset Boulevard.* Something happened during the second week and we never heard from him again. He closed his office and was gone. We hoped that he sold his film, but we never found out. We later heard a rumor that he "fell off-the-wagon." This business can do that to you.

Since we were too late to participate in AFM's screenings, we needed a place to screen our films. Ala *Cinema Paradiso,* we decided to project our films on the outside of our hotel every evening at dusk. There was just one problem – a big spotlight shined on the wall exactly where we wanted to premiere our films. Problem solved – I held Sarah by the legs as she hung over the roof's edge and unscrewed the bulb.

One evening as we were showing one of our films, a producer from *Life Is Beautiful* stopped by to complement us on our creative inventiveness. We were surprised that the Santa Monica police didn't hassle us, since we had the projector sitting on top of Sarah's Explorer which was parked at a meter on the street – with no money in it. We attracted quite a crowd. In fact, a reporter from the Santa Monica Bay Weekly wrote an article about our resourcefulness.

- *Santa Monica Bay Week*

   "The Other American Film Market"

   by Jessica Overswise

   Sarah Reid, a native Texan and Brendan Shepard, originally from West Virginia, both in their mid 30's, decided they had had enough of corporate Hollywood and three months ago formed a partnership in a company they call Amazon Films. They placed an add in the Hollywood Reporter inviting new scripts, shorts and finished films, which they promised to take to the Cannes and American film markets to sell. The response was overwhelming.

After carefully going through each submission, they settled on three films and marched over to the Lowes Hotel on Ocean Blvd. in Santa Monica, which is currently hosting, for nine days, the largest film market in the world. Unfortunately, the hotel was totally booked. Undaunted, these bold and enterprising entrepreneurs went directly across the street to the modest Ocean Lodge Hotel, rented the front suite and set up shop.

Manager Daniel Gregory allowed the women to put up a large banner that said, "The Other Film Market" across the front of the building which directly faces the Lowes, along with signs soliciting buyers with

free champagne and cigars, to view their videos.
Gregory said, "These are two gutsy ladies who believe
in themselves and are making happen what they set out
to do."

The plan was to have three gorgeous girls in
skimpy Amazon costumes, and on Saturday night, stand
outside the Lowes and pass out flyers to the crowd.
They never showed. The women had to create another
way to get attention, so they parked their Ford Explorer
in front of their hotel and placed a tape deck and
projector on top of the car and projected one of their
films directly on to the exterior of the Ocean Lodge
Hotel. Shades of "Cinema Paradiso."

Brendan and Sarah say that they have been
received mostly with respect and "lots of people have
responded to our fearless and fresh approach by giving
advice and helping with much needed contacts."

One distributor said, "You two are a breath of
fresh air in this stuffy film market." Their portfolio
states "In a town and an industry that has become very
corporate and unapproachable, unless you have an
agent, lawyer, priest or rabbi in your back pocket,
"Amazon Films" is attempting to tap into the talent that
Hollywood lures, and then ignores." On last sighting,
they said they have a "possible couple of foreign sales
on two of their projects."

That was just the beginning of our marketing ploys. Next, we
hired an actress/stuntwoman, Carol Mott to dress up as an
Amazon woman and parade around Loews. She looked exotic,
athletic and sexy in a chamois loincloth outfit carrying a seven
foot spear that Sarah had bought back from a trip to Africa.
We couldn't believe that Loews let her in the hotel with that
menacing spear. She passed out cigars and our invitations to
visit with us during our happy hour. Of course, she got a lot of

attention and created quite a stir in the jammed-packed lobby. In fact, every day E! Entertainment did a TV segment from there and one day they interviewed us about independent filmmaking and our renegade approach to the AFM.

Brendan, Carol and Sarah

Carol Mott, spear and Hollywood Icon, Angelyne

One company, who was trying to sell films, actually asked us to join them in their suite at Loews to help promote their films too. We graciously passed on the offer. We were feeling confident, and we felt that we were well on our way to making our presence known. All we needed was one little thing - someone to give us money for our film. With all of the people we met and took to lunch, how could we fail?

That was something we learned quickly – Hollywood loves to "do" meetings over lunch. Most of them materialize into nothing. We began to meet people for coffee. Again, thank you, Starbucks.

Hollywood is also about parties. Deals are done at parties – but usually, no one can remember what they promised. At AFM we went to party after party. Some we were invited to, and others we crashed. At one memorable soirée we were chatting with a distributor from France and up walks a business associate of his. After a lengthy discussion about giving us a pre-sale for our movie project, the associate suggests that we do a threesome. Since there were four of us standing there, I wasn't sure who the odd man out (or woman) was. We politely excused ourselves from the conversation. That's the thing about needing money – it's hard to be rude to the potential supporter, even if you want to scream, "Get lost, you scummy asshole." We ran into them again at another party where they had a couple of wannabe actresses cornered.

One of the best parties was thrown at a Santa Monica bowling alley. An actor we had recently met, Cole Rust (who was the official Elvis impersonator of South Africa) invited us to the party and gave us a name to use at the door. Apparently, there were a limited number of invitees that each guest could invite. We showed up late, but not too late. We found out the next day that our "Elvis" friend arrived at the party after us and discovered that we were the last to enter on his list. Hollywood loves lists. And bouncers, doormen, or whatever they're currently called, love to turn away non and late listees. They wouldn't let "Elvis" in. Sorry, but that's showbiz.

To our delight, a couple of publications ran articles about us during AFM. The LA Times even did a feature article about us. They called us the renegades and referred to us as guerilla producers. All in all, they were very positive articles and brought more attention to Amazon Films.

- *Los Angeles Times/Our Times (Santa Monica)*

"How to stand out in a jungle" by Deanna Welch

Flaunting an unruly hairdo and shredded, brown leather clothing, Carol Mott hardly fit in with the movie industry crowd milling around with cell phones, dark sunglasses and tailored suits.

Dubbed "the Amazon Queen," Mott, a stuntwoman and actress in her 30's, created a stir in the lobby of Loews Santa Monica Beach Hotel on Tuesday where entertainment industry executives congreed for this year's American Film Market. The "suits" repeatedly strolled up to Mott, taking the free cigars she offered and spouting curious questions about her attire.

It was the reaction Brendan Shepherd and Sarah Reid, two savvy businesswomen who sent Mott out into the lunchtime crowd, had hoped for. After she

drew them in with the costume and cigars, Mott told the

industry moguls about Reid and Shepherd's company.

Late last year, the pair started their own film

production company, Marina del Rey-based Amazon

Films. Using a jungle theme, they decided to make a

splash with the approximately 7,000 film industry

executives from across the globe there to wheel and

deal for overseas screening rights of about 300 films.

Amazon has become one of the big buzzes at the

market. To catch the attention of the hordes of movie

dealers, the pair projected the movies they hope to sell

on the wall of the Ocean Lodge hotel across the street

from Loews.

"How dull to go to all these screening rooms,"

said Shepherd, who has worked for numerous

entertainment companies. "We decided to do

something different...So we're touting ourselves as the

renegades. We consider ourselves the OFM-the Other

Film Market."

    Armand Gazarian, producer of Westlake

Village-based Tamseal Entertainment Companies, saw

one of Amazon's screenings and may distribute one of

its movies.

    "What they did really caught my attention,"

Gazarian said. "What they are doing is great. This

business is ruled by too many men."

    Producer Ray Nailog said the Amazon Queen's

presence caught a lot of attention and maybe a lot of

business.

    "She is eye-catching," he said. "It's a great

idea."

    And for Shepherd and Reid, they say

they have done a lot of networking and feel that their

company is off to a strong start.

"We'll definitely be back next year," Shepherd said.

Today is the last day of screenings at the

American Film Market.

AFM was expensive, but productive. We met tons of people, got our name out there and found a distributor for our films that we represented. The question was – what next? It seemed logical to attend the next festival which was the Cannes Film Festival in May. We thought surely we could complete the deals we had pending there...

SARAH

Cannes, France. Wow. The ultimate film festival, or it was back in the hey-days. Now there are so many trendy spin offs. It's cool to be in Sundance where the hip, young new-comers are; and Toronto is a fast growing festival that seems to be quite respectable. Venice, Italy has gotten bigger in the past years due to the fact that anything Italian is trendy, rich, and full of life. But still, nothing compares to Cannes.

We had already made our entrance into the festival world with a big "That's Amazon Films" at the American Film Market. And as AFM wound down, we heard others say it, so we said it too, "See you at Cannes." It was just two months away.

BRENDAN

Somewhere during AFM we had decided that we would not get involved with the distribution deals for the films we represented. Each of the producers agreed that they would cut their own deal. That probably was a mistake. Even though we made somewhat of a name for ourselves during AFM, we could have used the money, no matter how little. We were spending our own money and using credit cards to fund our business, in hopes of recouping it all in the near future.

Sarah and I had created a solid business front. Both of us were organized. We incorporated Amazon Films immediately and even trademarked it. Unfortunately, we did not get amazonfilms.com – Amazon.com already had it. (We always meant to talk to Jeff Bezos about that). We opened checking

accounts, had credit cards in the business' name and hired a

team of entertainment lawyers to create legal documents for us.

We had been introduced to a well known entertainment lawyer,

Harris Tulchin who we wanted to work with, but after a brief

meeting, we all agreed that he was beyond where we were at

the moment. We really did want to work with him, but figured

that he was way too expensive for us. We told him that

someday in the near future we would work with him. But not

now.

Note: FIND MONEY FROM SOMEONE,

SOMEPLACE, SOMEHOW. TRY NOT TO USE

YOUR LAST DOLLAR.

3

A STAR IS BORN. 1954.

Directed by George Cukor.

Starring Judy Garland and James Mason.

Tagline: "Is the price of stardom a broken heart?"

BRENDAN

Harris was introduced to us by a writer friend of mine, Martin

Zweiback who had written a couple of screenplays that had

been produced a few years before. One, with Katharine

Hepburn and Nick Nolte, *The Ultimate Solution of Grace*

Quigley was highly praised. I had known Martin for a while,

so I knew that what he wrote was good, but he seemed to be

upset when we weren't interested in pitching his scripts. They

simply weren't what we wanted right at the time. I discovered

that keeping business and friendship separate can be

complicated.

SARAH

We specifically wanted to work with writers who were not difficult. And we wanted to give those writers opportunities that weren't available in this town. In fact, in our publicity, we always talked about the wealth of talent available in this town, but no way to access it unless you have an agent, lawyer, rabbi or priest in your back pocket. We wanted to work with people who didn't have big attitudes. We just wanted to get our first project off the ground.

BRENDAN

After discussions with C. Dickson, the writer of *The Martini,* Sarah and I decided that this was the script we were going to put our efforts into. Although it was a first draft and needed work, it was still pretty funny. We were happy that we had product to pitch.

SARAH

Brendan and I agreed that we would keep our writers in the loop. After AFM, we continued to call and update the writer of

The Martini about all of the things that were happening with the project and what we were doing – because we were really excited about our progress. We told him when we had a director attached, when we had gotten actors and when we decided that we were going to the Cannes Film Festival. One day we called to tell him about some new development and he flatly told us to call his agent. I was pretty shocked by this. Just out of the blue. We had thought that by keeping him informed on everything, he would be excited too. This was his story and it was a good one, a fun one. One that we believed in. In an elevated voice I asked him why he felt that he had to have an agent. We already had an agreement. He again said to call his agent and hung up. I was furious. I called him back. Sometimes yelling at someone can't be controlled. "Who do you think you are? This script was going nowhere before we took it."

It was true. We were the only ones interested in the script and we had been up front and honest with him from the very beginning. Brendan was a little pissed at me for talking to him like that. She didn't want to burn any bridges, but I was so angry that he had done this to us. Several days later we went to see his "agent" - a guy named Tony, who lived and worked out of his apartment above Sunset Blvd in Hollywood. He represented minor league baseball players and was obviously a jack of all trades lawyer.

Of course, we were all a little on the defensive as we sat down at his kitchen table. He told us that he was representing Dickson and that he now wanted a $2500 option fee, which was equivalent to the Writer's Guild Union Rules. Dickson wasn't even in the Writer's Guild. He also wanted money based on a sliding scale of the final budget, i.e. if the movie was made for $3 million dollars we would have to pay a certain amount of dollars and if the movie was made for $5 million it would cost us more. He insisted upon five percentage points in the movie. He wanted way more than we thought he deserved. The final thing was that he wanted to be guaranteed a starring role in the film! We were just flabbergasted.

Now it was our turn to let Tony know what really was going on. We both told him how Dickson had seen our ad in the Hollywood Reporter soliciting for screenplays, shorts and finished features; and how we met with him and what we discussed. Dickson even acknowledged how no one else was really interested in it. In fact, all he had was some actor from a soap-opera who wanted to direct it. No one of importance was attached; maybe he had some backers at one time, but the money obviously fell through. We told Tony how we had gone out on a limb to put this project together and gotten people interested in it; and again we reminded him of what we agreed upon. We told him that we didn't have an agent either. When we all made the deal, it was simply based on trust. We told him that we had been so excited about the project and confident that everything was ok with Dickson, that we didn't think that we had to rush a written contract. And by getting an agent without discussing it amongst us, it was like being stabbed in the back.

We had stupidly kept Dickson abreast of every detail involving what we had been doing. I guess the publicity that we created about his screenplay went to his head. If he thought he was getting any money out of us up front - we didn't have any. There was none to give.

After I finished telling our side of the story, Tony looked us both in the face and said "If you're bullshitting me about this, I'll make sure you never work in this town, or I'll take you down." As if that made us afraid. But we did end up paying Dickson a thousand dollars for a six month option. It was money that we desperately needed. I wanted to deck him.

BRENDAN

One of the biggest mistakes that we made in our early days of business was not getting our agreement in writing with Dickson. He was a first time writer, never had an agent and never had anything produced. When we first met him, he was politely quiet and grateful to have anyone look at his script.

When the deal went sour, I was boiling inside, but I didn't want to fuck it up. We had already put a lot of time and money into *The Martini* and we were on our way to Cannes with it. He had us over his barrel.

We sort of knew from the beginning that his real desire was to star in the film in one of the best roles. But when we asked him for his acting reel, he had nothing to show us. He told us that in the five or so films he was in, they cut him out for various reasons. I could see maybe two or three times landing on the cutting room floor – but five? Red Flag! Red Flag!

Nevertheless, we were willing to keep an open mind about another lesser role. But I didn't think that he had a Kevin Costner/*Big Chill* future (His scenes were cut out in final edit).

We almost walked away from the script. We didn't though. We were forced into an agreement that we felt was beyond what he deserved, and truthfully, it took away some of the passion I had for the project. But we reminded ourselves that "This is Hollywood."

Sarah was determined to make Dickson see the error of his ways and reminded him time after time of his verbal agreement – as a "man of his word." This just pushed him further into a corner and it was a matter of time before he started striking out at us. I guess we played "good guy, bad guy" without planning it. I really just wanted to hurt him too. And I'm truly surprised that Sarah didn't.

SARAH

We were on our way to Cannes within two weeks, where we believed that we would easily make a sell and be shooting by the fall when the option ran out. At the end of October, we could purchase the option for another six months for $2500. We signed and said, "Fine." Deal done. But I will never forget what Dickson did and I think that put bad mojo on the project. I never talked to him again. We never again told him anything that we were doing on the project. We walked away learning a big, expensive lesson on this one. We were so innocent and naïve, thinking that we could share all of our excitement with this writer.

Many, many writers who crossed our paths thought that their project was the only one that had ever been written. It was amusing how once we appeared to be interested in their script, all of the sudden, they didn't want to let go of it.

Another writer had gotten Brendan's name from a friend and sent us a script, which we really liked. We spoke on the telephone and met with her several times. Finally, we asked her to sign an agreement with us giving Amazon Films a one year option on her script. But she wanted to include a list of restrictions. We had been down this road before and weren't going there again! We really wanted to pitch this project, but we were ready to walk away from it. We challenged her by asking, "How many screenplays have you written?" Her response, "Eight or nine." "How many people have called and met with you and have been interested in taking your script, putting their own money to print copies and promote your writing?" "No one." "Then make a choice. You have eight other scripts if we take this one. That's the deal." She signed. On the other hand, we had a writer who is every producer's dream. My grandmother had been put into an assisted living home in Gonzales, Texas and I wanted to get a Yellow Pages book from this small little town so I could order her something from time to time - flowers, candy, etc. So I called the local Chamber of Commerce in Gonzales, Texas. I was talking to the lady who answered the phone and said I would like to get the local Yellow Pages. When I finally gave her my name and started to give her my address she said, "Is this our Sarah Lea Reid? Gertrude's granddaughter?" I had grown up spending many weeks each summer with her daughter Carla. So we laughed and talked and she sent me the phonebook.

A few months later I received a phone call from a woman named Mayron Ellis Cole. She said she had grown up in Gonzales, Texas and her mother had always told her if she ever had a question, to call the Chamber of Commerce. (Wouldn't that be a great ad for the Chamber of Commerce?) Mayron had written a script and didn't know what to do with it. I find this funny because she is an accomplished musician with a music publishing company of her own in Houston, Texas, married to a well-known orthopedic surgeon. But she still called Gonzales Chamber of Commerce (population of maybe 5000 on a good day) to ask what she should do with her script. She started talking to the Chamber of Commerce woman and when she told the woman her name, the woman responded, "Is this our Mayron Ellis? Well, this is Bradly Farmer."

After all the pleasantries, Mayron said, "I've written a movie script and don't know where to send it." Bradly responded, "Well, I know someone in LA who's a producer."

Mayron called and asked me to read her script, *Welcome to Da Nada*. I informed her from the get-go that we are just two women working out of our homes, trying to put this company together. I told her that I would read her script and let her know where I thought she should send it, or what she should next do with it. I just wanted to make sure that she understood that if she sent it to us, she wasn't sending it to a big studio like Universal or Paramount. She understood completely. I also told her to give me a couple of months to read it because we had stacks of scripts to go through. Since we put the ad in the *Hollywood Reporter*, and by word of mouth, we had so many scripts that Brendan and I had divided them equally to read. Most were badly written, which is to be expected, but we found a few gems that we truly fell in love with - the stories were in some way, magical. Just like *Da Nada*. I could actually visualize the productions and could see the movies taking place. The scenes. The locations. I just knew they would be interesting to a large audience. Mayron's was one of those. When Brendan read it, she agreed that it was a good, funny story.

When we called Mayron back and told her that we wanted to pitch her script, she was ecstatic. We also let her know that because we started our company on a shoestring, we didn't have any money, and would she be interested in letting us option it for one dollar for a year. (We were learning that things take longer than expected).   She was more than

delighted. So we faxed our very basic contract to her which we

had taken from the Writer's Guild guidelines.

We had many conversations with Mayron over the next few

months. It was wonderful to talk to her. No one had validated

her writing before. We were confident that someone would

like it as we did, but we were also realistic - we were really the

ones taking the risk and again investing our time and money on

unknown writers. Mayron, from Gonzales, Texas was an

unknown.

Someone must have told Mayron to find a lawyer. I got a

phone call several weeks later from a woman with a law firm in

Houston, Texas who began drilling me about things in the

contract. That was fine, but she wasn't being very pleasant

about the whole thing, and there was no reason to be nasty.

At one point I began to get a little put out with her arrogance and challenged her. She began to back down a bit, but my feathers were already ruffled. The lawyer also faxed us a lengthy contract that she wrote with all kinds of clauses and stipulations – plus, she wanted a big option fee, which we didn't have. She told me that Mayron hadn't even sent this around to other studios. I agreed with her and said then she should certainly send it out.

I spoke to Mayron a few days later about the conversation with her lawyer and she was stunned. She said, "I'll call you back."

About 20 minutes later, Mayron called back and said, "Sarah, I just fired that lawyer. I'm so sorry. I really didn't know her. She's just arrived from LA where she was an agent and had just joined the law firm that represents my music publishing company. She kept telling me I should send it to other people, and I kept telling her that I wanted you girls to have the script.

I'm going with you." I said, "Mayron, we are small time. Maybe you should send it around first - I completely understand." She said, "No way. I want you girls to have it."

The first place we thought to pitch *Da Nada* was at the Hallmark Channel. They thought it was pretty good, but they said they weren't doing any "period" pieces at that time. They sent back a very professional and nice rejection letter. I faxed it to Mayron, who said that she just couldn't believe that we thought it was good enough for Hallmark. "I'm going to frame this next to my option check for $1.00."

She had the same reaction when we talked to NBC and other places where we pitched it. She knew we were working hard to get the script out there and she really appreciated it. That's the type person we wanted to work with. Pleasant, appreciative, helpful. We were all in this together. It would only benefit us all, but it was fun working with someone like

Mayron. She did lots of re-writes for the script and we kept her informed on what we were doing because we knew it was exciting for her. We also trusted her, and she trusted us. A great relationship. I still hope and believe that someday we will get this off the ground. Thanks Mayron!

Note: GET IT IN WRITING – IMMEDIATELY!

4

THE WIZARD OF OZ. 1939.

Directed by Victor Fleming.

Starring Judy Garland.

Tagline: "Follow the yellow brick road..."

BRENDAN

After all of the crap we went through over *The Martini* we took

deep breaths and moved forward. Cannes! We're really going.

Getting ready for Cannes was exciting. To attend the film

festival was always one of my dreams. So here it was, coming

true. We bought our airline tickets immediately, even before

we had a place to stay. We called everyone we knew who was

going to the festival to see if they had an extra room. Then a

few days before our departure, Sarah attended a friend's

grandmother's funeral and the friend knew of a place in Cannes that had just been remodeled and the owner wanted to rent it out during the festival. We rented it two days before we were to leave. And got it for an unbelievably fair price too.

Now, everyone in Hollywood knows that you need to have great clothes for the Cannes Film Festival. So for the week before we left, Sarah and I bought stuff. Long gowns, short cocktail dresses and suits. We shopped everywhere from Loehmanns to Neiman's searching for the best deals. And we found them. We were sure that we would look good for both meetings and parties. These were a couple of the additional expenses that we did not budget for.

Note: LIFE'S FULL OF ADDED EXPENSES -

BE PREPARED

SARAH

Cannes, France? I'd always heard about it; I had been within
30 miles of it when back-packing through Europe just after
college, but I'd never been. I looked on the map. Simple
enough – a coastal town. I thought, like Los Angeles. Now
just how do we get there?

Brendan was, and still is the more superior of us on the
computer. She found all the information online about
registration for the festival. Only $750 dollars per company for
three main passes into the hotels and events, and you could also
bring along three escorts to the screenings. We thought,
"That's pretty reasonable." We were trying to talk our director
on *The Martini,* Deran Sarafian into going with us as our third
person. We filled out the forms and sent them in, Deran's
included. We were late as usual and had to send them by Air
Express in order to get our names into the book. Book? What
book? But we were assured we would be registered.

Now what else do we need, besides money? My money was running a little low. I had been divorced for almost a year. My wedding ring wasn't doing me any good, so off I went to the jewelry mart in downtown LA to sell the diamond from my wedding ring. My ex had purchased it in South Africa when he was on a shoot there, so I knew even though it wasn't that big of a diamond, it was of fairly good quality. If I could get half of the value, I would be happy. I knew he had paid around $3000 and when I was offered $1500, I took it. Money from Heaven - for Cannes.

So we were headed to Cannes, we were registered and we were taking one script - *The Martini* to pitch at the festival. We had a few people attached - entertainment lawyer Harris Tulchin (yes, he agreed to work with us), director Deran Sarafian and a few actors.

Harris called us one day and asked if we wanted to help host a wine tasting party at the *Variety* (as in *Variety Magazine*) tent. In this gigantic white tent, you can find information on everyone at Cannes. You can also eat there, get trade magazines, and use computers to check your email.

Harris knew someone who had started a Wine Country Film Festival and was taking cases of California wine over to Cannes to promote this California film festival. We called the guy, Steve, and he told us that he could even get us a wine called "Martini." How fabulous. We found these great little cocktail napkins that had a martini glass on them and we had "Amazon Films *The Martini*," written on them.

Perfect. We were on our way to the Cannes Film Festival (with nothing but a script) and we were already hosting a wine tasting party at the Variety Pavilion.

But where would we stay? It didn't matter - we were going to Cannes! We were only a couple of weeks away and still without a place to stay. We had booked our flights, but the hotels were either way too expensive or way out of town, or all filled up. But things were just falling into place for us.

A week before we were ready to leave, my neighbor's ninety-six year-old mother passed away, and while attending the funeral, I saw the grand-daughter, Carrie Rickey, a film critic from the *Philadelphia Enquirer*. I expressed my condolences and Carrie said to me, "Oh, Mom tells me you're going to Cannes." I talked with her about what we're doing. She asked me where we're staying. I replied, "We don't know, but even if we have to stay in the train station and change into our ball gowns in the toilets, we're still going." She said that she knew someone in Cannes who had an apartment and gave me the phone number of this lady. Of course, we called, faxed and sent our money immediately after talking to the woman. It's in the Miramar Palais which doesn't really mean anything to us, but as we tell people over the next week where we're staying and how much we're paying, they are in disbelief. Mostly, because of the location and low price. Some people are staying in tiny apartments five blocks away from the beach for twice as much as we are. This place is right in front of the ocean and we're paying $2000 for 10 nights. *And* the apartment had just been refurbished. Everything was new - the couches, the kitchen, everything.

INCREDIBLE. Things were once again just falling into place for us.

BRENDAN

Sarah and I made our travel arrangements with different airlines. She went American and I took Northwest. We couldn't get a good fair to Nice because it was last minute, so we decided that we would take the train from Paris to Cannes. I wanted to stop in Paris for a couple of days, so I went early. Amazingly, unplanned, we both jumped out of taxis the same time at the Gard Nord train station in Paris. Sarah's suitcase had broken somewhere in her travels and she was having a difficult time pulling it. She kept hitting people with this huge suitcase as it toppled over. I laughed at the image that popped in my head - the Beverly Hillbillies showing up with their possessions hanging off of a wagon. I helped Sarah a little, but I was loaded down – all of those party dresses.

Once we were settled in our seats on the train, we glanced around to see if anyone looked like they had money. Always thinking about pitching. Why in the world would "money people" be taking the six hour train when they could fly into Nice, which is minutes from Cannes? We didn't think about that then. We were just so excited.

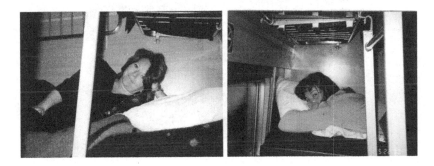

Exciting train ride to Cannes

SARAH

Our trip to Cannes was filled with lots of anticipation. What would we find? What would we do? How did this whole thing work?

We arrived exhausted, took a taxi to our hotel and now actually realized why everyone else had ooed and awed when we told them where we were staying – in the middle of everything. The Miramar was on the oceanfront walk.

Miramar

Cannes poster

View of Cannes from church that we never attended

We could step out our door and be right on the Croisette - in the action. Oh, my Gosh, we were really here. We hurriedly checked in and wanted to just get outside and walk. There were thousands of people walking around in the streets and the energy was high as people were arriving. You could just feel the level of excitement and anticipation that good things were going to happen. People had come here because they loved movies. They were here to sell their dreams and there were actually people here to buy them.

BRENDAN

Our hotel was in a semi-circle design, and as we unpacked, relaxed and prepared to head out on the streets, I went out onto the balcony and looked down a couple of floors. To my shock *and* delight, on the other end of the curve was the most beautiful man I'd ever seen. I was sure that he was a model or a European actor, and he was drying his naked body off in front of his open balcony door. I couldn't help but watch the show. He was looking around and saw me watching him, but continued. When I called Sarah to come look, he would step back inside behind the sheer curtain that was blowing in the slight breeze. Once Sarah went inside, he would come back out in full view. He was really putting on a show. I thought this must be the best place ever - we arrive in Cannes, stay in a great location, have a newly redone apartment to live in for two weeks and a beautiful naked man appears out of nowhere. Starting off right. I thought to myself, "I love Cannes."

SARAH

Naked, schnaked! I never saw the guy. Brendan was hallucinating on Cannes air. But she stood there long enough. She must have been looking at something.

Off we went to see what else was happening. We walked up

and down the Croisette, into some of the glorious hotels. You

know they must have been lavish in back in the 40's and 50's.

It was so wonderful - just to stand and look. The beach is on

one side of the street and the hotels line the other, facing the

ocean. Here we were. In Cannes. The French Riviera. Cote

d'Azur. On the Croisette. At the Cannes Film Festival.

Now what? How do we get started?

Someone we met on the train mentioned to us that you have to

register and pick up your pass and bag. We arrived at the

registration area and stood in line. Of course, we had to ask

everyone for information on everything, since we had never

been here before. After we signed in, we picked up our

picture badges.

Brendan and my pictures were pretty good, but Deran's photo closely resembled a terrorist. We looked in the "Guide" (the Cannes Market Guide) to see our photos and the very little information about Amazon Films that we wrote. We didn't know anything about this book, so when we filled in the application, we just put in the basic stuff. We didn't realize that all of this would go into the guide and that everyone would see our photos and the lack luster description of Amazon Films. We would know better next time.

Participating companies at the festival had their offices at the big hotels. Every room in each hotel was completely filled by production companies, distribution companies, etc. No wonder people were amazed at our location. The last hotel, the Majestic at the end of the strand was almost across from the Palais – that's where the premiering films of the evening were shown. This is where the celebrities would arrive, exit the limousines, and strike dramatic poses on the red carpet for photographers – pictures that you always see in *People Magazine* showing the fancy gowns the actresses are wearing.

It's the first day of the festival. We blindly trot from room to room asking if we can pitch our project. We kept getting "They are not available, come back later. Blah, blah, blah." Then Brendan asked just exactly how did we get to see these heads of the companies if they were always busy? One of the sympathetic assistants told us that we needed to make appointments in advance and that they would usually listen to pitches toward the end of the week, after most of the distribution deals had been made.

BRENDAN

I could see the writing on the wall. We were not making any headway. Sure, it was exciting and everyone was more than polite, but we were losing precious time. Just dropping in wasn't working. We needed to do something – quick!

SARAH

We created a different strategy. We spent the next couple of

days pounding the pavement, (and I do mean pounding - my

feet were aching!) setting up appointments and meeting people.

We also found out that the Majestic was the place to go for

cocktails at the end of the day. So around 5pm or so, we would

wander over there and try to meet people.

One thing that helped us get appointments was our "stress

balls." We had small balloons printed in LA that said *Amazon*

Films, Sand from Cannes. We actually sat on the beach two

mornings in a row and filled about 200 balloons. They were so

heavy in our bags, but we would carry those around with us

everyday. The secretaries and assistants loved the stress balls.

We had several say, "Oh, yes; you're the girls with the balls."

We would just laugh. It was a gimmick that worked, and they

remembered us for that. And we got appointments.

After we were in Cannes a few days, we finally found Harris,

our "believe in us" lawyer.

When we showed him our list of appointments, his eyebrows

raised. I think he was really impressed that we had lined up

almost 100 appointments over the next few days. They were

booked 30 minutes apart, so we tried to book the close ones in the same hotel, otherwise we were running up and down the street - which we did a lot of anyway.

Harris looked over the list and decided which ones were important. He would join our meetings for those. Harris was a real trooper. He wasn't really too sure about us, but he seemed to be amused at our naiveté and our enthusiasm at the same time. That was the same with Deran, our director. They really believed in us – that we could do it!

When we first started giving our pitch, we were a little unsure of ourselves. After a few pitches, we began to get the hang of it. People loved the pitch. Both Brendan and I were extremely animated in our delivery and every time we did it, we exaggerated it even more.

The entertainment business is pretty much a male-dominated business and the men really loved hearing a pitch from two

"Southern Belles." We were often told that we were a breath of fresh air to this stuffy, too serious crowd. While we were serious about what we were doing, we also had a great time, and were really just tickled to death to be at the Cannes Film Festival. Some people work in the movie business all their lives and never have the opportunity or the guts to do what we were doing.

We discovered that another good way to get into see someone for a meeting is by giving out invitations to a party. So we passed out invitations to our wine tasting party at the Variety Pavilion.

The party turned out to be great. And tons of people showed up. It was a late afternoon party and the "Martini" wine actually showed up from California. Harris hooked us up with a couple of United Airlines flight attendants who were on an overnight to help us serve it. They were fun and stayed until the last person left.

At the party we met this guy, Michael M from Canada who had a dot.com company. He took a liking to us and invited us to go to dinner with him and some of his board members. He said that we were enchanting. And we were. Or we thought we were.

So off we went to dinner. Already in the taxi that picked us up is Carl Bott, a former producer for a LA based Japanese company, Largo Entertainment and Michael's assistant and his girlfriend. The taxi took us up to the top of Cannes to a beautiful and quaint restaurant, Le Moulin de Mougins. We are told that it's one of the best places to eat in Cannes. We sat

at a round table and the ordering begins. Aperitifs.

Champagne. We had lobster appetizers, lobster salad and more

lobster. Then the meal came. We laughed, ate, talked some

business and had a great evening. Carl introduced us to several

people as Amazon Films, two women who are about to make

their mark in the film business. We were being equally

included in true "Industry" discussions. After dinner, we

wanted to take a picture in front of the restaurant, but Carl

didn't want to be in the picture. The taxi driver subtly

whispers, "His wife might see it."

We liked Michael. He was interesting and pretty cool. After

that evening, we saw Michael at other parties and one night he

invited us to a party on a yacht off shore. It belonged to some

Arab prince, I believe. A woman whom I had previously met

from one of the distribution companies asked if I was with

Michael. When I said, "No," she replied, "Good, cause you know he's married." He forgot to mention that.

BRENDAN

Michael was fun and exciting, but I knew something was up with him. He was a little too smooth for my instincts. It hadn't occurred to me that he was married. After all, no ring. When he asked me to go on the yacht, I begged off. He tried to entice me with the prince thing. There was only one prince I cared to meet and he was probably somewhere other than on a yacht, singing "Little Red Corvette." I wasn't going on any boat out into any ocean with any other prince of any kind.

Finding out that Michael and Carl were both married made me wonder if the business discussions were real, or if Sarah and I were simply being hit on. Just maybe.

Note: DEAL OR NO DEAL?

I loved being in Cannes, but I wasn't having *that* much fun so far. I was exhausted and I could barely walk, my feet hurt so much. I wasn't getting much sleep and really didn't feel like flirting with men to get a film made. All in all, at this point I wanted to be at home, but I kept on. The possibility of taking home a distribution deal was like a carrot dangling in my face. So we continued to pitch, pitch, pitch.

SARAH

One time, we were pitching, and I had been out the entire night, came in at six am, slept two hours and then got up at eight for an appointment at nine am. I was a zombie, to say the least. As we walked into the meeting, we introduced ourselves and I sat down. Brendan started the pitch and Harris arrived just after she started, but stayed in the doorway listening. At some point about halfway through, why on earth she did this I'll never know, she turned to me, who was sleeping with my eyes open, acting like I was listening and said, " Sarah, why don't you take it from here."   I turned my head and looked at her. I had no idea what she had already said. I was zoning out. Several seconds of silence passed as everyone stared at me and then Harris, realizing I had no idea where Brendan was in her pitch, literally leaped into the center of the room and continued the pitch. Well, I was awake by then. After we said our goodbyes and walked out of the room, we all broke into laughter. I had learned my lesson - actually listen to what the other person was saying, even if it was the ninety-ninth time I had heard that pitch!

BRENDAN

Sarah doesn't remember that I was out with her until six am. I started out the pitch ok, but then I went blank. My eyes glazed over and I shook myself back into reality to keep from falling down. My exact words were, "Sarah, you're so good at this part, why don't you take it from here?" Only retrospection really makes it funny.

Note: LISTEN, LISTEN, LISTEN.

5

BIG NIGHT. 1996.

Directed by Campbell Scott and Stanley Tucci.

Starring Stanley Tucci and Tony Shaloub.

Tagline: "In love, in life,

one big night can change everything."

BRENDAN

Sarah was single when we went to Cannes. I had a boyfriend whom I lived with. He wasn't keen on me leaving for two weeks, and was real unhappy that I was taking eight party dresses to the South of France. I guess it's difficult for the one staying behind. He should have known me better - I was strictly about getting a deal. The entertainment business is a very social business and loved ones who are not involved in it sometimes feel left out. It's also hard for *outsiders* to distinguish between the difference of work and play. What

87

looks like play is generally very hard work. Sometimes
there's also an amount of jealousy coming from someone who
has to work everyday at a job that they don't particularly like.
That's why you see so many people in the film business
marrying each other. They also get divorced.

SARAH

The nights were incredible. Just what you always hear about.
How can anyone stay up all night and work all day? We
learned fast that contacts were made at these parties and deals
initiated, so we had to go.

You also met interesting creatures of the night. We met this
weird, but fun guy named Paul. He kind of latched on to us.
He had a *People Magazine* that he carried around which had an
article about how he crashed parties. But there was his picture
in this magazine with every celebrity imaginable, Sylvester
Stallone, Arnold Schwarzenegger, etc. He actually was a lot of
fun.

BRENDAN

He told us that he was rich and owned a hotel resort outside of San Diego. When we got back to the states, I looked him up and indeed, he owned the resort and that next year I saw him on some TV dating show that featured eligible bachelors who were millionaires.

I've often wondered why we didn't hit him up for money for our projects. We just didn't believe him, that's all.

When we wanted to get into a party without an invitation, we would wiggle our way to the front of the line and say we were with Amazon Films and hand out a stress ball. We always got in.

SARAH

One night we went to the MTV Slamdance party. It was the hottest party that night and everyone wanted to go. It was crazy with young aspiring producers and directors and it was *the* place to be. The party was on the beach, but while we were waiting to get in, some thug-looking Frenchman grabbed my boob. I slapped him, and he turned around and sucker punched me in the face and I went flying back onto the ground, cute skirt and all!   All of the guys standing there jumped on him and beat him up a little. Brendan helped me up and they immediately let us into the party.

BRENDAN

I remember it clearly. Sarah had on this great looking black cocktail dress and an expensive silk chiffon shawl that I had loaned her; and suddenly there she was lying on the hard cement – with my shawl wrapped around her face. I pulled her up to her feet and dusted her off. After the shock, we both began to laugh. I gave her the shawl to keep.

SARAH

This was the year that *The Blair Witch Project* was released. No one had heard of it yet, but there were these flyers on what looked like notebook paper, asking "Have you seen this woman?" on them. Their dot.com address was at the bottom like a phone number so you could tear it off. The flyers were in a couple of hotels and nailed to several telephone poles around Cannes. You didn't know what it was. We just thought someone was really missing. But by the end of the festival everyone was talking about the film and how great it was.

BRENDAN

It was a brilliant promotional campaign by Artisan Entertainment or whoever did the publicity. The film was ok, but the intrigue that Artisan created made the big bucks for the company. I don't think that anyone has promoted a film since that's matched *Blair Witch*.

SARAH

One afternoon I was walking down the Croisette and passed Carl Bott. He stopped me and said that he was going to the AmFar Aids Charity Party that Elizabeth Taylor hosted and suggested that I go. He told me that tickets were usually $2500 but some seats were still available now for only $1500. Such a deal I couldn't resist. I'm in. I'm here in Cannes and I may never be here again. I have a credit card and I gotta go. I'm going to a party with Elizabeth Taylor! So I sign up, and this shopping bag arrives at our room with confirmation of my ticket and all sorts of goodies: Chopard perfume, Ray Ban sunglasses, chocolates and other things - I'd never seen anything like this before.

BRENDAN

As I try to nap before the next cocktail party, Sarah comes rushing back to our apartment all out of breath and tells me that she is going to the AmFar Party. I say, "Great" and try to fall back to sleep. Then she tells me how much it's going to cost. I literally jump out of my bed and scream at her that Amazon Films cannot afford it. She pacifies me by declaring that she used her personal credit card. I just rolled my eyes and went back to sleep.

SARAH

The next day I got my ticket. I'm thrilled. Carl says to sign up

to sit at his table, which I did. Then, I needed to fix myself up

in Hollywood fashion, so I made appointments to get my hair

and make-up done. Everything started early for the event, but

we were still pitching our project until about 4:30 pm. I ran

back to the apartment to shower and get my dress and then

rushed to the Majestic hotel for my hair and make-up

appointments. The salon is hurrying to finish, but I impatiently

thought, "Now I'm late. Dang. The screening of the film

started at 6pm and it's 6:15. My gosh, I paid all this money

and I may not even be able to get in!" As my last eyelash was

curled, I threw on my dress and literally ran towards the

theater.

BRENDAN

I happened to be window shopping through the streets of

Cannes during this time. And who do I see at the end of the

street with her gown hiked up in her hands running like mad, first in one direction and then in another? Yes, the one and only party Diva, Sarah.

SARAH

The theater is still a few blocks away and most traffic is blocked from the area. The only vehicle in the vicinity is a garbage truck; so I flag him down and he drives me right to the red carpet entrance. I hop out of the truck, adjust my dress and fluff up my hair; and with my new Ray Ban sunglasses on, walk up the red carpet in front of a crowd of on-lookers. And all of these people begin to applaud me. They think I'm one of the celebrities. So I give them a little princess wave back and keep walking. It was fun and pretty exciting.

The first person I see on the inside of the theater is Harvey Weinstein of Miramax. I tell him that Deran Serafian says hello. He says to me, "Oh, you know Deran?" I reply that Deran is the director on our film. We chat a bit and he says that we'd talk later. I go into the theater where Carl has saved

94

me a seat. The movie *My Life So Far* with Colin Firth was okay, but definitely an "art film" which I thought would probably not make much money in theatrical release.

During the credits at the end of the movie someone mentions that there are buses that will take us to the next part of the event. I say, "Buses?" "This is a good thing," they explain. "We can drink all we want." This whole crowd of people in tuxes and gowns pour onto these large tour buses that take us outside of Cannes. As we arrive, the first thing I see is a big white tent. I'm told that this is where the silent auction items are being displayed.

When I got off the bus, there are what looks like, a hundred paparazzi taking pictures. Another red carpet. Now I'm getting good at this.   I walked really slowly because Salma Hayek was in front of me.

The cameras were flashing all over the place and I stood fairly close to her, hoping that I would get in one of the pictures. It would have been too obvious if I had gotten any closer.

 **ME** ➡

When we walked into the tent, there were celebrities everywhere and very expensive French champagne was flowing. Now, it was still early in the evening, so I'm trying to pace myself; but after two hours of sipping champagne and not eating many of the fancy hórderves, I'm feeling pretty good. I've already walked around a couple of times and looked at all of the items being auctioned, so I bid on a few things. I just wanted to put Amazon Films' name in places that would be seen. I never really thought that I would be the winning bid. In fact, on two items, I was the *only* bid. Very few people were bidding on anything - that should have been my first warning as to what was to come. I "won" a silver necklace for $400 designed by Margo of Manhattan. I also bid and won a haircut with Jose Eber (Elizabeth Taylor's hairstylist). Another $500. I'm $900 in the hole but not feeling so bad. These I can cover. The haircut with Jose Eber would be a deal because I know his price is about $1,500 for a personal haircut and consultation. I had never heard of the jewelry designer, but I recently discovered that she has jewelry that is being worn on some popular TV shows; so what I paid for it was actually a steal.

I walked around for a couple more hours. When I ran into Carl, he introduced me to everyone who passed us. He was really considerate in that respect. He always made sure that Amazon Films' name was mentioned and made us sound like we were on our way to big success - which we felt we were.

Carl said to one of the editors from *Variety* and *The Hollywood Reporter*, "Let me introduce you to a woman from Amazon Films who is really moving forward in this business, doing great things; you should do an article on them."

When it was time for the live auction, Carl and I saw that there was a barrier and about seven rows of lawn chairs set in a semi circle around the front of the small stage. A few seats were still available, but they were roped off; you had to pass a security guard to sit down. I started moving towards them and told Carl "Come on," but he stopped to ask the security guard if we could sit there. The guard said, "If you're bidding." Not missing a beat, I replied, "We just might" and kept walking toward the empty chairs. Even though there were pieces of paper with names on them in the seats, we sat down. The champagne continued to arrive. I wasn't yet tipsy or slurring my words, but I was certainly feeling pretty good and a lot less inhibited.

Harvey Weinstein was the master of ceremonies for the evening. After a long wait, Harvey finally announces the arrival of Elizabeth Taylor and escorts her to the stage. Just amazing - here is someone I've seen in movies or on TV all my life. Someone from my Mom and Dad's generation, always on the covers of those old movie magazines that my grandmother had in her house when I was young – where I spent my summers in the big city of Dallas. Cameras are taking pictures of her at every angle. Harvey introduces her again (like she needed to be introduced) and suddenly all of the lights go out. And they were not suppose to. It was a weird moment. There were all of these celebrities sitting there in this tent, along with some very valuable jewelry and other priceless things - including Elizabeth Taylor in the dark, on the stage. The paparazzi cameras started flashing like crazy which gave off some light, but it was about two minutes before the lights came back on. Security and bodyguards, who suddenly appeared in the crowd from nowhere, started jumping up on the stage.

When the lights came back on, Harvey didn't miss a beat. He began the auction by donating $15,000 for Ben Affleck to come on stage and salsa dance with Salma Hayek. Everyone loved it. There were tons of expensive items up for auction. One was a wildlife painting by Peter Beard, another was an old 1952 Mercedes painted by Japanese artist Hiro Yamagata and a letter from Greta Garbo's private estate. The Mercedes went for a couple of hundred thousand dollars. But other than that, I actually thought everything was going at a pretty low bid considering the wealth in the crowd.

Cinema Against AIDS
Live Auction Catalogue

Diamond Choker Necklace: 66 square cut diamonds set in
18 ct white gold
Courtesy of CHOPARD

Diamond and Gold Elephant Pendant Necklace
Courtesy of CHOPARD

"Flamingo," a fully restored and hand painted
1952 Mercedes-Benz 220A Cabriolet
from Hiro Yamagata's Earthly Paradise collection
Courtesy of Hiro Yamagata

A Dress from Princess Diana's collection designed by Catherine
Walker from her 1992 State Visit to Korea
Courtesy of Alby P. Maccarone, Jr.

Ray-Ban sunglasses designed by Martin Katz with lavishly applied
brilliant cut diamonds, pink sapphires, rare Paraiba tourmalines,
Mandarin garnets and green Tsavorite garnets
Courtesy of Ray-Ban

"Hunting Cheetahs on the Taru Desert" and
"Orphaned Cheetah Cubs"
two signed photo montages by Peter Beard
Courtesy of Peter Tunney

A Letter from Greta Garbo's Private Estate, written to
screenwriter and friend, Salka Vertal
Courtesy of David Wolkowsky

One Half-Hour Private Tennis Lesson with Chris Evert
Courtesy of Chris Evert

One Hour Private Tennis Lesson with Pete Sampras
Courtesy of Pete Sampras

One Hour Private Tennis Lesson with John McEnroe
Courtesy of John McEnroe

One Hour Private Tennis Lesson with Monica Seles
Courtesy of Monica Seles

One Hour Private Tennis Lesson with Steffi Graf
Courtesy of Steffi Graf

One Hour Private Basketball Lesson with Pat Riley
Courtesy of Pat Riley

Then, in comes the Princess Diana dress from her State visit to Korea. The dress is on a mannequin standing on the side of the stage. When they carry it to the front of the stage, it looks like they're carrying a dead body. As they plop it down, Harvey seems to recognize that the whole scene feels uncomfortable, so he yells, "Elle, come on up and put this dress on." He's asking super model Elle McPherson to put it on. Then he says, "A million dollars for Elle to put this on right here." Of course, no one bids on that, but she does go off and comes back with it on.

To the side, standing behind the roped off area, probably because I'm sitting in his seat, is a man from South Africa who's been bidding on almost everything. I saw that he bought the Mercedes and some famous oil painting. So every time something of value comes up for bid, everyone turns around to see if he's going to bid on it.

Harvey begins the auction on the dress, "OK, let's start the bidding at $55,000. Now, he's looking over to the right, the opposite direction from where I'm sitting. I slowly put my hand up by my face, no higher than my head and look in the direction of the South African, just as everyone else is.

Suddenly, Carl shouts, "Harvey, over here" and points to me. Harvey looks around at the crowd and swings his extended arm towards me and in a voice that will haunt me the rest of my days, shouts, "Fifty-five thousand dollars to the girl in the third row." I slowly turn my head back around to see who he's talking about. With complete shock and in one of those "Lucy" moments, I realize that he's talking to me. My hand goes down and for the next three minutes which seems like eternity, I'm in shock. Carl doesn't know that I've sold my wedding ring to get to the Cannes Film Festival. Carl doesn't know that Amazon Films has no money. Carl doesn't know that I just finished my fourth glass of champagne. Inside my brain, I'm going, "Oh, my gosh, Oh, my gosh, Oh, my gosh."

Harvey keeps asking for the next bid, but no one was bidding,

and I was dying inside.

In my mind, I was thinking that I could turn around and sell it

on eBay for $150,000 to some rich Texan for his wife or to an

oil Baroness, and I would make a profit of about $100,000.

But how do I get out of France tonight? How do I pay for it?

Will my Amex cover $55,000? I also envision myself in the

dress, homeless on the Promenade in Santa Monica with a sign

that reads, "Take picture with the Princess Diana dress for

$5.00!" I am sweating bullets now. Harvey is making small

talk about the dress to get other bidders, but no one else has bid

on it. My wheels are still turning in my head, when I hear

Harvey shout, "Sold for $65,000. I am truly dying. Carl turns

to me and shouts, "That's the gutsiest thing I've ever seen

anyone do." I am sober and silent for the rest of the night.

After the auction, Carl and I are standing in line waiting to be

seated for dinner. Carl is telling everyone, "She bid on the

Princess Diana dress, she bid on the Princess Diana dress."

I'm not yet basking in the moment. I'm still shell shocked.

The woman in front of us turned around and asked me if I was

the winning bid on the Diana dress. Carl pops in, "No, but she

bid on it and really wanted it." Yeah, right - if he only knew.

The woman was from the *London Times* and said that she

would like to write an article about me for the paper. Brendan

and I met with her the next day and we chatted a bit about who

Amazon Films was, minus the fact that we didn't have $55,000

for a dress or anything else. There didn't seem to be a writing

angle for an article in a British paper that was interesting even

to us. She said she was looking for something with more of a

lighter side and we were seriously pitching Amazon Films.

She never wrote the article.

The party was over. The goody bags were great. Chopard was one of the sponsors of the party, so even though there wasn't a big diamond necklace in them, there was nice perfume. There were a lot of wonderful things in the bags. I remember a red, white and blue Tommy Hilfiger wind jacket, and I got two pairs of Ray Ban sunglasses. Those bags are valued in the thousands of dollars. I've comforted myself in knowing that my $1500 ticket to the party wasn't all in vain.

I went back to our apartment, jumped on Brendan and woke her up. It was about 5am and she didn't comprehend much until I told her, "I just bid fifty-five freakin' thousand dollars on a Princess Diana dress!"

BRENDAN

It was like someone threw cold water in my face. All I could say was, "No, you didn't, no you didn't." Sarah was shaking me. "Yes, I did, yes I did." Finally, the image of Sarah raising her hand and Harvey swinging his arm around to her was picture perfect in my head. I sat up, fully awake now. Again,

"No, you did not." Sarah just laughed and laughed, "Yes, yes."

Thank God I didn't go to the party. I would have had a heart

attack. In fact, just hearing the story made my heart beat faster.

When I got over the shock, I started to laugh. I really would

have loved to have been there for that moment. I'd like to

think that somewhere Diana is also getting a giggle out of the

whole thing.

Sarah continued to tell me every other detail of the party. After

the dress story, all I wanted to hear about was the goody bag.

They were the buzz in Cannes. Everyone knows that they are

fantastic.

After we finished looking through her loot, I wanted to know

who "important" was there and how they looked.

SARAH

Besides, Liz, Ben Affleck, Salma Hyatt and Elle McPherson, there weren't tons of stars. I talked to Elle for a second. I knew that she just had a baby, so I asked her how the baby was and she sorta blew me off. I was just being polite, Elle. Val Kilmer was there. He's a good looking guy. He wasn't talking much to anyone. I'd heard a rumor (which most are based in some truth), through the production grapevine that on his movie *The Doors* a memo was sent around to cast and crew telling them not to make eye contact with Val or speak to him unless he spoke to them first. Really, Val.

Actually, there weren't that many people at the event. I'd heard that the ticket sales were down. In fact, they are usually $2500 dollars and they were reduced to $1500. I'm not sure why they didn't sell.

For me, everything after the AmFar party was anti-climatic.

BRENDAN

Except for one of the last evenings in Cannes when we ran into a distributor, Mickey P. from Strom Entertainment. It was his birthday and at 8pm he smelled of old alcohol and was already not standing up straight. When he saw us, he gave us big sloppy kisses and asked if we would come up to his hotel room and give him a blow job - since it *was* his birthday. I jokingly said, "Only if you give us a distribution deal." He slurred, "Ok, we'll do the deal afterwards." I laughed with, "Deal first, blow job afterwards." Of course, we had plenty of invitations from other *"sober"* men to do the same and we didn't, so this was not especially tempting. The next day when we ran into him, he pretended (or maybe it was actually the case) he didn't remember anything he said. That happens even when they're not drunk.

6

THE PRODUCERS. 1968.

Directed by Mel Brooks.

Starring Zero Mostel and Gene Wilder.

Tagline: "Hollywood never finds a zanier zero hour."

BRENDAN

Returning from Cannes was an exciting time. Harris Tulchin

advised us not to take copies of our script to Cannes because

hardly anyone has time to read them there. So we got into high

gear two days after we returned to LA and sent over fifty

scripts to the distribution companies that we had pitched to

who were potentially interested in our project. We couldn't

afford a delivery service, so we delivered them ourselves.

Sarah drove her Explorer to each and every place, usually

parking illegally, and I ran upstairs with the delivery. If I was

dressed in something better than jeans and tee shirt, I would ask for the recipient personally. If I looked a little too casual, I passed as a delivery jockey.

In Cannes, every company's office was either at the Carlton, the Hilton or at the Majestic Hotels – all were beautiful. But in LA we were able to see who really had the money. A few companies were in top notch areas and had stunning offices, but some were in run down buildings that looked pretty shabby. Of course, some of those companies with high rent offices are no longer in business and the less than elite film companies are still around.

Along with the scripts, we included a PR packet. There were bios, cast list, published articles about us and anyone involved on the project. Deran Serafian had committed to direct a couple of our films before we left for Cannes. Deran had directed several large budget movies for studios (*Back in the USSR*, *Terminal Velocity*, *Death Warrant*), but was willing to do our film for scale. He had just come off of Warner Brothers' canceled project, *Flying Tigers* where he was a play or pay director. That simply means that he gets paid even if the movie doesn't get made. So he didn't need the money.

We also had commitments from Tony Curtis, James Gandolfini, Yasmine Bleeth, Chris McDonald (*Thelma and Louise, Family Law, Quiz Show*) and a basically unknown actor, Evan Adams who starred in a wonderful Miramax film, *Smoke Signals.* We were also trying to get Jamie Lee Curtis for a role. We thought it would be cool for her to perform with her father. We sent her a script and talked with her agent several times, but it never materialized. They politely recommended calling when there was money in the bank. We were never sure if she even got the script or knew that her father was attached to it.

We had met with one of the top casting agents in LA, Mike Fenton (*E.T.*, *Close Encounters* to name a few) and he liked us. He was working with Deran on the *Flying Tigers* film before it was cancelled. He liked Deran too. That's probably why he met with us.

He and Sarah established a quick rapport because they were both runners (She's run in several marathons); but bonding wasn't enough to get him to work with us. Simply put - we needed money in the bank before he would contact any actors.

Everywhere we went with our script, we were told a variation on cast. Some said, "If you bring us George Clooney, we can do something. Others said, "Who's Yasime Bleeth?" And of course, Evan Adams meant nothing to anyone but us. We quickly discovered that cast is very important.

We did have a rep at Miramax who was pushing to get *The Martini* to production. Apparently, he loved Tony Curtis and wanted to do a film with him. Sadly, the rep went somewhere else (not sure if on his own accord) and no other rep was as interested. After his sudden departure from Miramax, we couldn't locate our TC admirer. Just fell off the earth.

We weren't so naïve not to understand that if we had George Clooney or John Travolta we wouldn't need any of them. We could go anywhere and get our project funded.

How did we know that? We had already met with a couple of banks that gave loans for film projects. Lou Horowitz was one. We met with a vice president, Brenda Doby who wanted to help us, but we needed to have some "Collateral." Travolta would have been collateral. Getting money from banks is not cheap. We were told to expect to pay somewhere between 30 and 40% interest. Whoa. We about fell over until we discovered that if we went somewhere other than to a bank, we could pay 50% or more. Actually, we didn't care what we had to pay to get the money. But we still didn't have Travolta. That's a lesson that was hard to accept.

Note: CAST, CAST, CAST.

WITHOUT WELL-KNOWN TALENT, IT'S

ALMOST IMPOSSIBLE TO GET MONEY.

7

FROM RUSSIA WITH LOVE. 1963.

Directed by Terrence Young.

Starring Sean Connery.

Tagline: "Seduce. Blast. Strangle."

BRENDAN

Someone we knew had met a Russian woman who claimed to have money for film projects. "Yes," we screamed, "Get us a meeting with her." It was confirmed - Yelena would meet with us in a week in her home office in the valley. She had recently returned from Russia and was recovering from an intestinal infection that put her in the hospital for a month. We patiently waited for the meeting, but it was postponed for another week. Yelena had to have emergency gall bladder surgery. At the end of that week, Yelena had migraines. Could we meet the following week? Sure. We had just about given up on Yelena,

when she called us and said that she was now available.

As we drove up her driveway, we were impressed with the size

of the house. It sat on a hill in a suburban community of Los

Angeles, Northridge, overlooking the San Fernando Valley.

As we entered through grand double doors, we were greeted by

this tall and very large African American man who spoke in a

deep resonant voice. He introduced himself as Carlos,

Yelena's husband and asked us to wait for her in the living

room. Two furry yapping dogs followed close at his heals. He

closed the library doors behind him, leaving us in there with

the unfriendly dogs watching our every move. We stood

silently (Which is rare for me or Sarah) and looked around.

And there was a lot to see. Sarah and I were truly speechless.

The room was adorned with every kind of Russian (At least I

think they were Russian) antiquities allowed out of Russia – we

guessed that some were probably smuggled out – God only

knows why. They were so ugly. There were more ornate coffee tables than most museums had. And glass figurines sat on every table. Marie Antoinette women with painted lips and bulging breasts, men in knickers with white wigs, porcelain pigs squatting, sitting and laying on their sides. The several lamps went way beyond gaudy. It was really too much. I could barely look.

Both Sarah and I eventually sat down on an uncomfortable small settee and put our purses next to our feet. Just as we were starting to relax, the library doors flew open and in walks this short, over-weight, middle-age woman with iridescent orange hair. The two dogs rushed to her side. She shrieked at us to pick up our purses. She wept that if you put your purse on the floor, you will never have money. Sarah and I grabbed them up quickly (And to this day I will not put my purse on the floor). She ran over to us, hugged us strongly and kissed each of us on both cheeks, apologizing for her ailments. Then she proceeded to give us details of each illness. It was more information than we needed or wanted to hear, but we let her talk. During part of her diatribe, she cried into a nasty embroidered handkerchief and blew her nose loudly. She constantly said to us, "You can understand, can't you?" We both shook our heads "Yes."

After her final cry, she suddenly rose to her feet and invited us to see the house. All we wanted to do was talk about money, but our instincts told us to play along with this mad woman; perhaps this is how Russians do business. We didn't know.

Outside of the living room, the house was in pretty bad shape. The wooden floors needed re-varnished, the walls needed painted and the carpets were worn thin. Apparently Yelena didn't see this because she continued to ask us, "Isn't this place magnificent?" She pointed to a picture hanging on one of the walls. It was obviously of her when she was much younger and thinner. And it was quite nice. She told us that it was painted by a famous Russian painter who was commissioned by a Russian prince. She went on to say that the prince was her lover. She concluded with, "So was the painter." We fussed over it some, but started to open up the conversation about our film projects. Yelena waved her hand over her head in a circle and dismissed our comments with, "Plenty of time for money talk. Let's have tea."

Back to the living room we went. Again we sat down on the settee. After a few more minutes of us praising the house, in walks Carlos with a tray holding one of the most ornate porcelain tea sets I've ever seen. Also on the tray were these awful looking chocolate covered "Twinkies" that looked something like bad éclairs. They were wrapped in plastic and looked old. Sarah and I politely ate one. Yuck!

After a few sips of tea, Yelena started to talk about the projects

she was working on. Some were films, others were not. She

said that she could get us money for our film if she liked the

script. But she went on to say that she never reads scripts. She

called up some guy on the telephone and handed me the

receiver. She said that everything she does has to be approved

by this producer of hers. I talked to him briefly about *The*

Martini. He said that he would like to read it. We agreed to

send it to him the next day. Yelena said that if the producer

liked it, she would give us $5 million to get it made.

Then she went on to say that she needed $300 to initiate the

process. "The producer, he likes to get paid something for his

time." Sarah and I looked at each other. Now I was pissed. I

just wasted a whole morning with some shyster who had her

own scam going on. My comment to her was, "That's fine, no

problem. Just take it out of the $5miliion." Yelena squinted at

me, and then informed us that it was usually paid upfront; but she might have seen the fire in my eyes, because she continued

with, "I'll see if this time we can make an exception." Sarah

said, "That's the only way we'll do business with you." Were

we on our way to getting tougher? We sent the script to the

producer who liked it, but Yelena mysteriously disappeared.

She's probably in Russia buying cheap imitation antiques.

8

BOILER ROOM. 2000.

Directed by Ben Younger.

Starring Vin Diesel and Giovanni Ribisi.

Tagline: "Where would you turn? How far would you go?"

BRENDAN

Shortly after that, we were referred to a man, Pete who had a boiler room in Woodland Hills where he raised money for various businesses through investors. During our first meeting, Pete told us that what he did was probably not suitable for us. He worked with Internet, oil and gas and telecommunication companies. We disagreed, and convinced him to take a look at what we had. He was polite and agreed to listen.

Sarah and I always made a point to look professional at meetings. Some film producers go to meetings in tennis shoes and tee-shirts. We felt that if you looked professional then you were treated that way. At this meeting, I was dressed in a decent black suit with expensive leather shoes. However, when I got out of the car at the office building, I must have stepped in dog poop. I smelled something in the elevator, but there was someone in the elevator with us and I thought it must be them. As we sat in front of Pete's desk, I looked down at my shoe and low and behold, there was a little strip of poop hanging by a few dog hairs. Just as I looked up, it fell. Sarah caught my eye and saw the poop, but didn't miss a beat in her pitch.

Whatever Pete was saying, I couldn't hear. I was trying to decide how to handle the situation. What were my choices? Mention it and create a whole new conversation or let it go and hope that he thought it was someone else's poop. I quickly flicked it under Pete's large desk with the toe of my expensive shoe. I decided that the conversation between Sarah and Pete was going good; I didn't want to interrupt it with dog poop. After a couple more meetings, we convinced Pete that Amazon Films was going to succeed with or without him. Pete liked us because we had spunk. No one ever mentioned the dog poop. He said he'd take our project on if it was more than 15 million dollars. *The Martini's* budget was between $3 and $5 million (depending upon cast, distributor, our PMS, etc.), but we could certainly bump it up more with big name talent.

Unfortunately, when we were about ready to move forward on the deal with Pete, someone else came into our lives. And Pete had a heart attack and died. Not because of us, I don't think, but raising money is stressful.

9

GHOST BUSTERS. 1984.

Directed by Ivan Reitman.

Starring Bill Murray and Dan Aykroyd.

Tagline: "We're ready to believe you."

BRENDAN

Soon after Pete's death, we got a call from a woman who said
that her "advisor" wanted to meet us to talk about a project she
wanted produced. Sarah took the call and was curious about
the whole thing. I didn't want any part of it. It sounded too
wacky for me. A time was agreed upon and a meeting was set
up at the "advisor's" apartment. At the last minute I decided to
go. My curiosity got the best of me. When we arrived, a very
beautiful woman with flowing dark hair greeted us. She called
herself Rae Sun; she was the one that Sarah had spoken with on
the telephone.

We entered this very white room with white sheer curtains on the windows, the same white shear fabric hanging over everything else and white candles burning everywhere. It worried me that they were so close to the curtains. We sat on white pillows on the bare floor and I'm thinking, "Fuck, here we go again." After a few minutes, in walks an Asian woman in her thirties dressed in flowing robes, looking much like a Buddhist monk. She sat across from us and told us that she had been observing us at AFM and we were the ones she had chosen to produce her film project. After she finished talking, I guess I rolled my eyes a bit and asked, "How much money do you have?" Of course, I knew the answer. "None, right now. But we will be getting some soon."

Then she asked Sarah if she wanted her to do a reading. Knowing Sarah, I already knew that answer too. She took Sarah in another room and I patiently waited. When Sarah came out, there was an amused smirk on her face. Ok, I'm game. I went into the room with the woman and sat across from her on the floor. She asked me to relax and focus on her eyes. In a few seconds I felt calmer and then it blew my mind - I saw in her face an old woman's face. And it stayed there for at least a minute. Then it was gone. She asked me what I saw and I told her. She laughed and said, "You should pay attention to this spirit. She wants to tell you something." I was spooked. Before I left the room, I looked around in every corner for a camera or something to explain what I saw. I didn't say anything to Sarah until we were in the car. To this day, I try to figure out what I saw and how I saw it.

Nothing ever materialized from the meeting, but later in the year, I went for a massage at a spa in the Valley and the beautiful woman with flowing dark hair was now called Tiffany and she was the receptionist.

10

WALL STREET. 1987.

Directed by Oliver Stone.

Starring Michael Douglas and Charlie Sheen.

Tagline: "Every dream has a price."

SARAH

We were always looking for money. One day in the

Hollywood Reporter, we saw this add: *Venture Capital*

Available, Through Angel Investors. Let me introduce your

start-up company to a premier investment group. $7,000,000 –

invested this year.

Ok, Lookin' good. This was something we were going to

check out. We call the number and get this guy, Greg K. who

lives out in the San Fernando Valley somewhere. We set up a

meeting at his house which turns out to be this nice little

ranchette on maybe an acre of land. He has a couple of horses and a few chickens running around. So it's not an office in Beverly Hills; we're still ok with it. He tells us that he has investors in Santa Fe, New Mexico who have money to invest in film projects. He also tells us that we will be able to present our company to a group of about thirty of these investors. However – and there is always a "however" - it's going to cost us $2500 and we need to have a business plan. I called my brother-in-law who's a successful businessman and he said to me, "Sarah, you don't need to spend money to get money. You're trying to raise money." But did I listen to his wise words? No. I was bent on doing this. Here was someone offering us a chance to meet with people looking to invest their money!

So we put together a business plan and created a power point slide presentation about Amazon Films and our future goals.

Two weeks later, we're off to Santa Fe, confident that we are going to get money for our company. Of course, everything is being paid for out of our pockets – the $2500, which was paid up front. The airplane tickets, the hotel, the car rental and food. It all adds up to about another $2000.

The presentation is held at a very nice resort hotel in Santa Fe. Cocktails are served, and we meet several people, including the other six or eight presenters. Each one has a unique business idea he's pitching, but none have a film company. We watch a few of the presentations and are impressed with the great ideas. One was a dot.com that featured a website of entertainment, dining and shopping in cities around the nation. We thought his idea was the best – next to ours. He invited us for a drink afterwards and said that he would fill us in about this investment group. Uh, oh.

When the presentations were finished, we all sat down to dinner. After a few minutes of chatting, we realized that these people are not investors. There are some lawyers who are looking for new clients, and several business major students, observing. The rest must have been friends looking for a free dinner – at our expense.

Later, having drinks with our new dot.com friend, we discovered that not all is what it seems. First, he wasn't charged $2500 – his fee was only $1000. And secondly, there were not thirty investors at the presentations. We knew that. Actually, he tells us that there was only one real investor. Our new friend is from Albuquerque and has done more research than we did about the group. We are feeling stupid and getting pretty pissed.

When we returned to LA, we talked to Greg K. about the whole messed up thing. To pacify us, he said that he would give us a list of the angel investors who are part of this investing group. Never mind, that they weren't actually there for the presentation. He did give us the list and we started calling them. How many were still active members with money to invest? Around three. And they weren't currently investing.

Duped again. So we took Greg K. to small claims court for our $2500 – and won. He retaliated that the only reason we won was because the judge was a woman. Then he appealed, and back we went to small claims and we won again. It wasn't about the money. It was the fact that we were being hoodwinked and we were rather sick of it. We never got our money though.

BRENDAN

Sarah and I never stopped thinking about new ways to get our projects funded. We even went to the Small Business Administration to see if we could get a loan. Our meeting was with a consultant who was a retired film studio executive who worked with SCORE (Service Corp of Retired Executives).

His advice - find another business. One where we could put

our high energy into and get some reward. Both of us were

kind of surprised at his suggestion, but agreed that he was

probably right. But this is *our dream*. After convincing him

that we weren't giving up, he gave us information on raising

money through a DPO – a direct public offering. We had

already read something in the newspaper about them. He

referred us to Ace-Net. This SBA based organization set up

DPO's through a website. After filling out tons of forms, we

were accepted and officially did a public offering. We were

bound by certain restrictions. One was that we could only

accept 35 non-accredited investors. A non-accredited investor

is one who makes less than $250,000 per year or their net

worth is less than one million dollars. This is similar to a

private placement, but we were allowed to solicit investors. In

a private placement you must have a pre-existing relationship

with your investors. We were assigned a website address at

Ace-Net and investors could go to it and have a look at our business plan, our projects and who Amazon Films was.

11

JERRY MCGUIRE. 1996.

Directed by Cameron Crowe.

Starring Tom Cruise, Cuba Gooding, Jr.

and Rene Zellweger.

Tagline: "Show me the money."

BRENDAN

Sarah and I were a great PR team. We probably should have changed our business to public relations. Anytime something new happened with Amazon Films, we were emailing or on the fax machine sending a press release. Sometimes it worked. We would get calls back from newspapers or television stations. Most of the time, it was a bust. When you think about all of the press releases that go out on a daily basis, it's amazing that a small company like ours got any attention at all. At one point we met with a large PR firm in Santa Monica to ask them to take us on. When we told them everything that we were doing, their comment was, "Why do you need us? We wouldn't add much." The firm was owned and operated by two savvy and successful women who we liked immediately. Throughout Amazon Films minor peak of success, we kept in constant contact with the women. They actually referred us to Dale Olson who came out of retirement to do the PR for *American Beauty* with Kevin Spacey which won the Academy Award for Best Film. And everyone in Hollywood knows how important it is to have good PR to solicit the Awards.

Mr. Olson was a dear man and extremely successful. We were flattered when he told us that he would be seeing our names on executive desks someday. We liked him and were extremely happy that he wanted to help with our success.

As soon as we were approved for the DPO, Sarah and I began

calling magazines, newspapers, and any other publication that

would listen to us.

SARAH

We sent out postcards to multiple newspapers such as the New

York Times, Washington Post, USA Today, LA Times, etc.

with a picture of the two of us sitting on a blanket on the beach

as we talked on our cell phones and typed on our laptops. The

postcard read, "Yeah, We're different." And on the back it

announced our DPO.

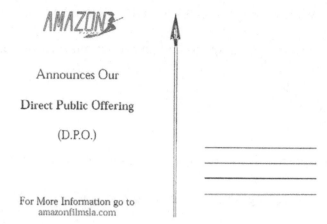

AMAZON

Announces Our

Direct Public Offering

(D.P.O.)

For More Information go to
amazonfilmsla.com

I followed up with phone calls to about 25 newspapers, but I

hounded the LA Times. We were locals, after all. They were

interested, but they weren't sure who should cover it. After

tons of phone calls, we finally were going to get another

article. The LA Times jumped in again and published a front

page article in the business section on us, picture included. It

basically was a good article about our DPO. But somewhere in

the second page there were these comments from someone at

the Sundance Institute. His exact printed words were, "They

have more chance of getting hit by lightning than raising

money for a film project this way." We thought that this was a rather odd and mean analogy.

And it seemed kind of weird that someone from Sundance would utter discouraging words about any independent filmmaker's pursuit to raise money. So long as it was legal. I wrote him a letter expressing our disbelief and displeasure of what he said, and after a couple of weeks we heard back from him. He said that his comments were out of context. Sure.

We continued to send out press releases. Now, it was, "What do Jeff Besos and Amazon Films have in common? Nothing, except the desire to succeed." No reaction from anyone.

12

THE STING. 1973.

Directed by George Ray Hill.

Starring Paul Newman and Robert Redford.

Tagline: "...All it takes is a little confidence."

BRENDAN

 We went to the Santa Monica library, sat there hours

befriending the drunks and homeless sleeping their afternoons

away. Going through the *Bacon's Book of Media Publications,*

Newspapers and Magazines , we got the addresses, phone

numbers and email addresses of any magazine that had to do

with business or money. We thought that if we could get

enough press, then someone would recognize our desire and

capabilities and give us money. I found a magazine called

Profit Magazine. They were in Palm Springs. Sort of local –

we gave them a call. It turns out that Jane Lanza owned the publication, and had started a company,

SHESGOTNETWORK.COM. Both Profit Magazine and SGN

were part of a parent company, Original Media, a publicly

traded company. And to make it better, they were looking for

women-owned companies to invest in. Oh, boy! Jane and her

husband, Joe Lanza just happened to be in Los Angeles that

week. It was suggested by one of the directors at the home

office in Palm Springs that a meeting take place. It was

arranged, and we met at Shutters Hotel on the beach in Santa

Monica.

Shutters is one of the best hotels in the LA area. Joe Lanza

met us there for the meeting. No Jane. He was a big guy,

tanned and appeared to be in his mid 50's. He was good

looking and charming. We took an immediate liking to one

another. When we asked about Jane, we were told that she had

"teeth problems" and had come to LA to get them fixed. Okay,

that seemed plausible.

During their two week stay, we met Joe a couple of times. He seriously talked to us about funding our projects. In return, they wanted us to create streaming videos and content for their website. We would oversee the entertainment division called SHESGOT ENTERTAINMENT. That sounded just fine to us.

At the second meeting, a couple of guys showed up. They had an idea for a company that they wanted to get off the ground. Their plan was to produce informational videos to show in hair salons. Educate the client while she was getting her hair colored. It sounded kind of bogus to us since most women want to be pampered at the salon, not educated; but we were polite to them just in case we later worked together. Yeah, we were naïve about a lot of things, but sometimes we had good instincts. We knew when not to burn a bridge. I knew, Sarah didn't care.

Every time we had a meeting, Joe would make an excuse for Jane not showing. We politely insisted on meeting her. She finally showed up at the fourth meeting. In walks this platinum blonde dressed in an outfit of faded designer jeans and a white shirt; and on her wedding finger was a flashy (what looked like) five karat yellow diamond. Wow. Sarah and I both took a second peek at the ring. It looked real. Jane was pleasant and enthusiastic in hearing what we had to say. We got along with her just fine, though we suspected that she might be on some kind of drugs. Her speech was sluggish and she lost her train of thought occasionally. It might have been the pain medicine the dentist was giving her. We never asked. But her teeth did look great.

We were invited to visit their offices at Palm Springs to further discuss a deal. We were excited, but cautious. Joe seemed awfully smooth to us and we really couldn't figure Jane out just yet.

The two salon guys gave us their cards and we called them the next day after our meeting. One of them had known Joe and Jane for a long while and told us that he and Joe had made a lot of money together in investments. We asked about the investments, but he was vague.

Coming from small towns, Sarah and I were mostly trusting, but living in Los Angeles for any time at all, makes you a little skeptical of people – especially people in the entertainment business. We just weren't skeptical enough.

The following week we met with Joe in Palm Springs. Their offices were quite nice and there were several employees on staff. Joe introduced us to everyone, and had his lawyer meet with us to discuss the specifics of the deal. It was an all day meeting and instead of taking a break for lunch, Joe ordered take out from a greasy fast food restaurant. Sarah and I both commented on it on our way home. He seemed like such a high roller in LA, but now we were getting second rate food.

For some reason this small thing unnerved me. It felt like a

"bait and switch." Never the less, the meeting went well.

They appeared to be as enthusiastic to have us on board as we

were to be on board.

It was agreed that they would buy Amazon Films and

properties and then employ us to run the division. As part of

the deal, besides the cash buyout, we would get stock in the

company, Original Media. At the time Original Media was

trading at about $10 a share.

Sarah and I were optimistic and hopeful that the lawyer would

have an equitable letter of intent for our next meeting.

Note: SOMETIMES, OPTIMISM IS REALITY'S

CHANCE TO FANTASIZE

Besides the greasy food, another thing that bothered me was Joe's "friendliness." It seemed that every conversation ended with some sexual remark. I let it go since we were so desperate for money. I hated that I felt that way. I looked forward to down the road when I could say something to him – once the deal was in place. Like, "If we have to listen to one more sleazy joke, you asshole, you're going to regret it."

SARAH

Right before this all happened with SGN, a dentist from Wyoming, Steve Cheek saw our DPO on the Internet and called us. Steve has an entrepreneur spirit and had a script that he wanted to produce with someone. He liked our spunkiness and decided that he would help us with our company. He referred his friend, a deep sea diver to us who was set to give us $25,000 to keep Amazon Films in business. It would have helped us tremendously, but when the Lanzas came into the picture, their lawyer recommended that we not take the money. Steve and his friend were disappointed that they were now out of the picture. We felt bad that we had to change directions, but we thought we were on a role with the Lanzas.

BRENDAN

At the next meeting in Palm Springs, we were given the letter of intent. Jane was at the meeting and we discussed the Cannes Film Festival. We agreed that we would go and promote the hell out of SGN.

SARAH

The letter of intent stated that they would send us to Cannes and when we returned, give us $750,000. $250,000 of that to open an office in LA and $500,000 to do our first "Internet" movie. Going home that afternoon Brendan and I screamed with joy. This was it! We'd been at this for eighteen months and finally got our big break. We were two weeks away from the Cannes Film Festival and these people weren't just telling us they could do something, but had gotten us two plane tickets to Nice and two tickets to the Elizabeth Taylor hosted AmFar party at $2500 each. Our dreams were coming true!

BRENDAN

The Lanzas worked a little slow for me and terribly slow for
Sarah. They would always agree to do things, then not do them
until we asked more times than was comfortable. The red flags
went up and down like flags at a NASCAR race. But we had
our blinders on. We were focused on making it work - and
going to Cannes!

Meanwhile, we took the letter of intent to Harris Tulchin to
evaluate. He made his comments quickly and we passed them
back to the Lanzas' lawyer. The deal was ok. Nothing was out
of the ordinary. We signed the letter and faxed it to SGN.

13

GROUNDHOG DAY. 1993.

Directed by Harold Ramis.

Starring Bill Murray and Andie McDowell.

Tagline: "He's having the day of his life... Over and over."

BRENDAN

Sarah and I came across an American real estate broker living in Cannes who found us a great place to stay. When I say great, it's an understatement. First of all, the apartment was on the Croisette right across the street from the Palais. The Palais was the center of the festival and where all of the big premiers take place. It's the red carpet with the many steps where you see celebrities walking up during the festival. We were on the fifth floor with a balcony overlooking the red carpet.

It was such a perfect view of what was happening on the carpet that we were asked by the BBC if they could shoot from our balcony. We let them one time. I don't think that they were particularly gracious, so there was never a second time.

Even though the apartment wasn't huge - it had one bedroom and a sleeper in the living room; it was plenty big for Sarah and me. From time to time, we even had guests stay over. We stocked the apartment with food and wine and enjoyed our time in it, even though it was limited. Luckily, we had Joe send a check for the entire rental – it was only $6,000. That's pretty good for Cannes during the festival.

We were still waiting on our airplane tickets. Joe assured us that they would be there. Sarah had to ask several times before we finally got them.

SARAH

Jane contacted a Hollywood publicist who got our photos and buyout announcement between Amazon Films and ShesGotNetwork into *Variety Magazine*. This was it. Our dreams were actually becoming a reality.

Femme portal buys indie house Amazon

By ANN DONAHUE

Indie shingle Amazon Films was acquired by women's portal ShesGotNetwork.com, it was announced Friday. The two companies will form a new entity, ShesGotEntertainment, which will develop film, TV and Internet projects.

Company will be led by Amazon Films producing partners Brendan Shepherd and Sarah Reid. Its first two Web projects are "The Estrogen Files" and "Flea Market Divas."

Brendan Shepherd, Sharon Reid

"We started out producing feature films and we started thinking about the Internet," Shepherd said. "We were looking for somebody to merge with, and when he heard about ShesGotNetwork we thought it sounded great."

Shepherd and Reid will promote "The Estrogen Files" during Cannes and will shoot a documentary of their experiences that will be shown daily on ShesGotNetwork. In addition, the duo will hype ShesGotEntertainment's first feature film project, "Welcome to Da Nada," which is slated to star Yasmine Bleeth and will be helmed by Deran Sarafian ("Terminal Velocity.")

Previous to founding Amazon Films in 1999, Shepherd worked at Buena Vista Home Entertainment. Reid worked in production for Universal and United Artists. ShesGotNetwork is headed by Jayne Newell-Lanza, who is also the publisher of Profit Magazine.

BRENDAN

Upon Sarah and my suggestion, SGN ordered 500 baseball caps with "Estrogen Files" on them. That was the name of the Internet show that had been developed by Jane. We also ordered a thousand flashlights with "SGN" written on them. Everything was last minute. Sarah and I were getting nervous about the slowness. Joe had ordered an HD camcorder and accessories for us to shoot the festival. The footage was going to be downloaded everyday on the website. For several days before we left for Cannes, we were told that the new camera was arriving at the office in California, but when it finally arrived, Joe said he needed it for something he had to shoot in Palm Springs. He said that they would ship it to us in Cannes via DHL. Not having the camera in hand when we left made us uncomfortable, since part of the reason for our trip was to shoot video for SGN.

Joe had a computer/video person, Johnny, working for him. Neither Sarah nor I knew that much about computers, but we surmised that Johnny didn't know much more than us. He acted like he did though. That was pretty frustrating because we never knew what he actually could do. He was a great bluffer. Before we left, we expressed our concern about the camera. Johnny assured us that it would get there. Sarah had given them the name of a company that had previously shipped camera equipment internationally for her. She mentioned several times that they should use them. When she shipped with them in the past, they always delivered without problems.

When we got to Cannes, the camera had not arrived. It was not there the second day either. Nor the third. Because it wasn't there the first day, we devised a plan B. We would find an aspiring director who brought a camera with him to Cannes and entice him into shooting for us until our equipment came. It didn't seem like an impossible plan.

As I was standing in the registration line for the festival, I met two young Australians. And sure enough, one was an aspiring director and he had a digital camera with him. The other was his friend, a medical doctor. I told them what we were doing and asked if they would be interested in filming for us. It was a match made in heaven. We fed them and they hung around with us shooting great footage.

Sarah and crew

After about five days, we discovered that our equipment from the states was "supposedly" being held at customs. They would not release it because the proper paperwork was not done. Joe did not use Sarah's recommendation for shipping. So much for our state of the art camera.

To make matters worse, the arrangements were not made to download and stream video. Before we left for Cannes, we had met a vice president of Intel and set up a meeting with Joe and him. We were told by Joe that everything was "a go" and they would be waiting for us in Cannes. Even though the Intel techs in Cannes didn't know anything about the streaming agreement, they were cooperative. Unfortunately, back in Palm Springs, they couldn't get it together. Again, plan B. We would overnight the footage, which we did. They still couldn't get it working.

Note: ALWAYS HAVE PLAN B

Before we left the states, we called our wine rep from the

previous year and arranged to co-host a party on a yacht with a

company called Filmbazaar.com.

During the party, we passed out our flashlights and talked

about SGN to everyone. It was a crazy but successful party.

That was a time when Internet companies were spending big

bucks on partying. And the partying was grand. Our

California wines were a hit. Later in the night the party got a

little wild and I was tired of talking shit, so I decided to leave.

I went looking for my coat in the stateroom and walked in on two women in the throws of passionate something or other with a guy. I wondered if it was the Frenchman.

Sarah and I were promoting SGN, but we recognized that there were some problems. So we continued to refer to Amazon Films as the production company. Whenever we talked about the projects, we mentioned Amazon Films as the producer. Initially, it was because we had pitched to many of the distributors the year before as Amazon and they remembered us. The difference was that this year we told them that we had money and that we would talk to them back home about what we were doing. It was incredible how much more interested they were in our projects.

Another problem for us was that we were not given any spending money. Joe promised that he would send us a cashier's check, but it came two days before the festival closed. And it was for half of what we agreed upon. We had been spending our own money, which we didn't have much of, and our reserves were getting low – and credit cards were getting high. For the entire previous year we had been spending our own money. Sarah had a commercial building in Texas that she sold and I had an investment property in Washington, DC that I cashed out; and I even used money from my 401K. Both of our credit cards were also getting maxed.

Note: NEVER GET RID OF REAL PROPERTY MAKING REAL MONEY

We weren't particularly concerned since our deal would allow us to pay back all of our debt. Also, I had been trading stocks and it was a time when everyone and anyone could make money in the market. I was up a considerable amount, so I wasn't panicky about paying off bills. Sarah and I split all of our expenses down the middle. That worked for us because neither of us had much more money than the other one. But Sarah liked to order lobster and steak…

In our daily shooting schedule in Cannes we interviewed celebrities like Sheryl Lee Ralph (who hosted the Jamaican Film Festival party) and even Spike of the infamous Spike & Mike Animation Festival. I remember at one party when I first met Spike I flippantly asked him where Mike was. With a glint in his eye that said, "I'm going to make you feel real bad," he hoarsely whispered, "Dead." I didn't know that Mike had recently died. Whoops.

We enjoyed the production part of our trip. There was so much to shoot. We traveled the backstreets of Cannes getting interviews with some of the merchants and shop owners. One of our favorite spots was a chocolate shop. The owner had some famous designer create and construct a dress completely out of chocolate squares. It was beautiful and looked delicious.

We also hired a young French woman, Anna to assist us. She worked part-time at the chocolate shop. Anna helped us a lot – especially one morning when we sat down on the beach and filled 500 SGN's balloons with sand for stress balls. God, what a job. It was "Sand From Cannes" again. Just like last year.

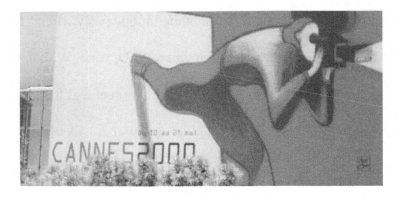

I felt that we were doing a great job in Cannes. Sarah and I kept moving forward, even though SGN dropped the ball. One evening before a premiere, we passed out our "Estrogen Files" hats in front of the red carpet at the Palais. They were definitely a crowd pleaser. In fact, we almost got mobbed. Of course, we got it all on tape.

Harris Tulchin was no longer involved with us on our project, but we hung out with him and rode around Cannes in his little yellow BMW convertible. One afternoon we drove to the Hotel Du Cap for lunch with him, a vice president of Porchlight Films and our two cameramen. The hotel is exquisite. It's about twenty miles east of Cannes on the winding coastal highway to Antibes, and is maybe the most expensive place to stay in the area. The grounds are lush with flowers and exotic shrubs and they only take cash. I have no idea why, but that's a fact. Probably the guests pay for everything on their credit cards at the end of their stay, but non-guests must bring cash. No Amex. No MasterCard. No Discovery. No Visa. Cash.

When we first arrived, we discovered that there was a press conference going on with George Clooney. We tried our best to get in, but we needed to have a security clearance and we didn't have time to get it. There were more bodyguards on the lawn of Hotel Du Cap than at the White House.

Lunch was an over indulgent, but delicious buffet. We sat outside on the veranda at a table next to Ethan Hawke and Uma Thurman, who were then still married. George Clooney and John Turturo sat two tables away, and Harvey Weinstein (Who was then half of the brothers Miramax) also sat close by. Our cameraman's name was Jeremy Weinstein and he felt brave enough to go up to Harvey as he picked over the buffet lunch. A French friend of ours who sat down to join us looked at Jeremy making his approach to Harvey and shook his head "No, no, not a good thing to do." We all sat quietly and watched.

Jeremy introduced himself and said to Harvey that he might be his long lost relative. Harvey was amicable enough until he saw that the "medical doctor cameraman" was filming him from the side of the veranda. To the best of our interpretation, his words were something like, "That's a #x$@&^-!* thing to do, get to #x$@ out of here." Jeremy walked back to the table totally destroyed. We all laughed about it, but it kind of ruined Jeremy's day. The thing that we noticed that no one mentioned beforehand was that there was this young woman along side of Harvey. I don't know who she was, and I'm sure that it wasn't improper, but we all agreed that it was a good lesson for the young Jeremy to learn.

Note: ALWAYS GET YOUR SHOT -
AT ANY COST

Actually, it was a blessing in disguise. Jeremy went on to get funding for a short film he titled, *Looking for Harvey.* I heard that he premiered it at Cannes the next year and I believe he received an award or two for it. I sent him the footage that we had shot for SGN so he could use it for his film with the request to return it; he never did. But, hey, that's Hollywood even in Australia.

While we lunched most of the afternoon, we observed the celebrities around us. George Clooney was outgoing and friendly to everyone. We agreed that he's a hot man. Real down-to-earth. Sarah followed John Turturo out of the restaurant as he was leaving and pitched him on *The Martini.* He was very receptive to her and suggested that we meet back in the states and talk about our projects.

Ethan Hawke was quiet and smoked a lot. He had his child with him and he was very attentive to her. We liked that. I don't think that Uma Thurman hung around much after she ate her carrot. Later that week, we saw her at a premier wearing a dress cut down to her butt and she looked more than fabulous.

The bill for lunch for the six of us was over a thousand dollars. Cash. That was our big splurge. But it was worth it. It was one of the best afternoons we spent during the festival.

The year before, I felt that we were on the edge of things, but this year it was different. Maybe because we knew so many more people and maybe because we thought that Amazon Films had a future. We were much more confident.

Towards the end of the festival is the annual AmFar party. It is the AIDS charity event hosted by Elizabeth Taylor, as in previous years. This year, Victoria's Secret was a big sponsor. The tickets went for $2500 each. And weren't discounted. And to make it even better, Sarah and I both went on SGN's ticket. Sarah wore a beautiful yellow full length gown from Neiman's and I wore a lavender colored gown that I bought on sale at Loehmanns for $50.00. We both looked pretty good. Sarah looked better.

Divas looking for garbage truck

Salma Hayek

SARAH

There was a cocktail party before dinner, then the fashion
show afterwards. The crowd was so thick that we were
bumping shoulders with everyone. We headed up to the bar in
the far corner of the room where there was more breathing
space. I looked around and there was Ivana Trump with her
tall dark handsome Count who she was dating at the time. But
they weren't even talking – just looking around. So here's that
moment, you either take a chance or the moment passes and
it's gone. We walked over and I introduced myself and
Brendan. I told Ivana about our new women's Internet show,
The Estrogen Files and she loved it. She said to call her office
when we got back to LA to discuss it further.

There was a silent auction at the cocktail party and everyone
was circling the center of the room where the auction items
were on display. When we made our way to take a look, Joan
and Melissa Rivers were passing us in the opposite direction.

Once again, I stuck my hand out, introduced us and told them about our women's Internet program. They also loved it. Joan said that she had recently launched a website herself and was really interested and said to call her when we got back to LA. We had just talked to two of the highest-profile women at Cannes and they were both very interested in what we were doing.

BRENDAN

Dinner was ok. Kind of like a wedding reception at the Four Seasons Hotel. Good. Very good, but not great. We sat at a table with our French friend from Hotel Du Cap and Miss Russia of a previous year. I sat next to a woman who was with a US rock singing group whose name I can't remember. She was friends with actress Mila Rostropovich (*The Messenger*). Mila spent more time at our table than she did at hers. She is a woman with natural beauty and is very approachable. It was like she had known us forever.

Sarah is the more outgoing of the two of us. She met people easily. I think that they liked her easy going Texas style. She kept bringing studio department heads over to our table to meet me.

As we were having dessert, I noticed that Ivana Trump, who was sitting close to our table, barely touched her food. We met her earlier in the evening and when she saw me looking, she gave a friendly nod in my direction. Actually, she looked great – much better than when she was with "The Donald." Her gown was quite elegant - a long chiffon dress that hugged her body. Her hair was not too puffed out as it use to be and her makeup was subtle. I was impressed by her attractiveness. She was classy and demure.

The Victoria's Secret fashion show was very artsy. Lot's of fog and feathers. Tyra, Heidi, Elle, Giselle and every other top model who is recognized by only her first name was on the catwalk. The theme was "Angels." Of which none of them looked like. If thin is truly in, then they all were cutting edge. Except Tyra – she's a full blossomed woman. We admired her figure. The models came out in mostly swimsuits and lingerie. Some were adorned with angel wings. It was an exciting show.

In front of us sat Gregory Peck and his lovely wife. I introduced myself to him and the couple was gracious as well as elegant. I think that of all the people I met, I was most impressed with Mr. Peck. No one can replace his grace and charm.

Behind the Pecks sat Jose Eber with his cowboy hat. Sarah had her hair cut by him in LA previous to our trip. She had won it in last year's auction at Cannes and finally cashed in on it. Jose appeared happy to see Sarah and told us that he had done Liz's hair. I wouldn't have admitted it.

Across the catwalk sat Joan Rivers. I had seen her close up at the cocktail party and had a hard time not staring at her plastic surgery when we were talking. It was a scary picture. The ever faithful Melissa was by her side as always. The two hosted E! Entertainment's Cannes segments which were actually pretty entertaining and funny.

Sela Ward sat there too. We talked to her afterwards. She is quite a beauty. It's wonderful to see someone so gorgeous and seemingly sane. Her back didn't have one roll of fat on it. I looked. And she's not an ingénue anymore.

Roger Ebert sat on our side of the stage in front of us. After the show I asked him what he thought of it. With a wicked twinkle in his eye, he said that he was thankful that Liz decided not to put on a swimsuit.

Ok, sure, Elizabeth Taylor was a little plump and shook as she spoke; but she still is exquisite. It was sad to see her so fragile. The woman is eternal and can do no wrong in my book.

Elton John looked hearty and healthy. He seemed to be having a good time. In fact, at one point during the party, Harvey Weinstein said that he would donate fifty thousand dollars if Elton got up on stage and played a medley of his songs - which he did.

After dinner there was the traditional auction. I bid on a dance with Prince Albert of Monaco. I started it with $3,000. Did I have that kind of money to throw around? Nah. I didn't think I'd really get the bid. I believe that he went for close to $10,000. Later in the evening I happen to walk by his table and told him that I was disappointed that I didn't get the bid to dance with him. At that part of the evening, I don't think he could stand, let alone dance. But he was extremely friendly and kissed my hand as only princes can do – definitely brought up to be charming, not sincere.

After the party, Sarah and I stopped by the Majestic Hotel for an after party drink. Nothing was happening too much, but we chatted with an actor from Greece. He was tall and handsome, but not too smart. We had never heard of any of his movies, but he carried around posters of them. His English was good and eventually he got around to talking about sex. He told us that he just had the most incredible love making session with an older Italian woman, an actress whose name we would know. No amount of prodding would compel him to tell us who she was. But he did give us the details of the sexual encounter. We had just met this man and we were getting way too much information, but we weren't bored. To tell you the truth, we thought he was gay.

Maybe he was, and was hoping that we thought his story was good enough to be made into a script. He kept asking if we had ever heard of anything like this before. Of course, we said, "Never." Just then, a very old man walked up to our table, politely greeted us and then turned to our Greek god and yelled something in Greek. It wasn't something nice. We could tell by the look in his eyes and how red his face got. Our beautiful man simply got up, bowed to us and left with the older man. We giggled on the way back to our apartment and discussed who we thought the old man was. His father? His lover? The actress' husband? We'll never know. But that's ok. We still talk about it and get a good giggle.

As we walked back to the apartment, the sun was just beginning to rise. We had no meetings in the morning, so Sarah and I walked down to the beach with our gowns pulled up over our thighs and sat down in the sand at the water's edge. We reminisced about the night and the days behind us. It seemed like a dream gone by quickly. It was a warm morning

and we stripped out of our gowns and went for a swim.

Walking back, we sang "I am Woman." Corny, but fun.

My boyfriend, who had flown over to Cannes a few days

before, was sitting at the dining room table drinking coffee

when we walked in. No amount of explaining could appease

him. After all, he was left behind. I guess it didn't help that I

came back at dawn. I can be shitty about it now, since we

broke up. Another LA relationship down the drain.

The rest of the week was kind of quiet. Although we went to

one last super party thrown by Working Title Productions at a

castle outside of Cannes. You had to take a charter bus to the

event and invitations were being checked in detail.

Apparently, the year before there were bogus invitations made.

It was amazing that invitations were checked so thoroughly

since there were about three thousand people at the party. The drinks were somewhat exotic – cosmopolitans, margaritas, etc. and continued through the night, but the food was pitiful. And, they ran out. I think it was mini hotdogs or sausage pigs in the blanket or something like that. Just awful.

There was a full moon and the outside walls surrounding the castle faced the ocean. It was a beautifully clear summer night and I had a great conversation with a distributor from a USA company which is now defunct. We chatted about how hard the film business was and what we really wanted to do. Both of us wanted to produce good quality films (Who doesn't), but we also understood how difficult that is to do. I sensed that he was moving on from the company he worked for. He'd been there several years and he said that he felt like he accomplished nothing.

SARAH

From the year before, we had tons of the *Martini*/Amazon Films napkins left over from our wine tasting party; so we took them to this party at the castle. We asked one of the bartenders if we could place them on the bars where people were getting their drinks and he said ok. Sometime about a half hour later, people started coming up to me and complimenting me on what a great party it was. I just said, "Thanks." We simply thought of it as recycling.

BRENDAN

As I was dancing my butt off at the party, I noticed Sarah talking to a handsome and intense-looking guy. I haven't paid much attention to any men not related to business; after all, I had a boyfriend and he was with me on this trip. But this man looked most fascinating. I walked up to them and introduced myself. He was Israeli and they were talking about war and how films portrayed it. He wasn't impressed with most of America's portrayal. He was a documentary filmmaker and was almost finished with his film about terrorism, which he planned to submit to the Academy Awards.

Here was maybe the best man we met at the festival. Good-looking, intelligent and sensitive to what was going on around him. Where was my boyfriend? I looked around and saw him talking to some blonde with a 44DD chest. Contrasts are some of the best lessons in life.

The entertainment at the party was great. There were a few bands who all played different styles of music. We especially like the hip hop group. They performed late in the night, so by that time, everyone was feeling no pain from their margaritas. One guy who danced next to us was getting a little out of control and practically knocked me over more than once. He didn't care what was happening; instead, he just shrugged his shoulders and laughed. The Israeli grabbed him by the collar, walked him to the gate and tossed him out on his ass. My hero.

No one even noticed the whole thing except me and Sarah –
and the invitation patrol at the entrance gate. There were still
people waiting to get in. It was 5:30 in the morning.

I thanked God that the parties were over. I don't know if I
could have made another 24 hour day. At least we had no
meetings scheduled for the rest of the festival.

The next day after the castle party, my boyfriend and I rented a
Fiat convertible and drove the coast of the Cote d'Azur to
Monaco and into Italy. It was a beautiful sunny day and the
mood was very romantic between us. We walked the
cobblestone streets of Monaco and drove the curving road
where the Grand Prix race was held the week before. The
bleachers and guard rails were still in place. It was thrilling to
be on the same road as the race. Monaco is one of the most
beautiful places I've ever visited. As I was sitting on a
concrete bench thinking about basically nothing, one of the

geeky distributors from the festival who was at our wine tasting practically ran up to me and started talking about how awful the festival was this year. That was the last thing on my mind. I took a deep breath and sighed way too long. He left without saying goodbye.

Traveling east we drove into the Italian Riviera. We loved the Italian countryside. France seemed so reserved compared to Italy. We arrived at a small town, St Margarita and fell upon a huge flea market. There were exquisite leather handbags, gorgeous cashmere sweaters and shoes, shoes, shoes. It was a feast for shopaholic eyes, so I bought a few things.

It was just about 2pm and the merchants began to close their shops. Time for lunch - which in Italy is at least two hours.

Italian Flea Market @1:59pm

We asked a woman on the street for the name of a good
restaurant. She pointed to a small café across from the beach.

Pasta, Arugula, Calamari, Wine

We had the best meal maybe in the entire time we were on the
Mediterranean Coast at this little place. Pasta with pesto,
calamari, arugula salad and garlic bread. The red wine was
smooth and we had a second bottle. The sun was starting to set
when we left. Did I say it was romantic? The best day ever.
And not a mention of the film business – except for the
Monaco troll earlier in the day.

My head started to clear of the festival and the past days. I was
beginning to relax a little. Maybe it was the wine. On the way
back to Cannes, my boyfriend and I stopped the car along the

coast, found a private cove and made love on the beach. What a day. I hated to go back to Cannes.

The Cannes Film Festival is a love/hate thing. The anticipation of going is great excitement. Being at such a beautiful place is almost overwhelming, but the intense wheeling and dealing takes its toll.

One week and two days into the festival, Sarah and I received a check for $1,500 from SGN. A little late and not enough. We were both ready to go home. We called the airlines and changed our tickets to leave the next day. We'd had enough. And we were anxious to get back to LA to move forward. When you want things to happen fast, they never do. Air France gave us a hard time about changing our tickets; then charged us an additional $80 each. To top it off, we were told that there were only first class seats available and there was an additional $200 per person charge. It didn't matter, we were ready to go. When we boarded, we noticed that there were plenty of seats left in coach.

We figured that we would settle the airplane ticket issue further down the line. All we cared about was going home and dealing with what our future might be.

14

MUTINY ON THE BOUNTY. 1935.

Directed by Frank Lloyd.

Starring Clark Gable and Charles Laughton.

Tagline: "A thousand hours of hell for one moment of love."

BRENDAN

There were so many unpleasant issues to discuss with SGN that we put off calling them for three days after we returned to LA. We still wanted the deal to work out, but it didn't look good.

SARAH

We finally went to Palm Springs after several phone calls of trying to get a meeting with Joe and Jane. Knowing that we were a little pissed off, Joe went on the defensive. He wanted to know why we didn't send them any media from Cannes. Brendan and I were ready. First of all, we *did* send tapes. Then we listed all of the issues that were directly related to

SGN's incompetence, from the promise of Intel setting us up for downloading our videos to not getting the camera.

Joe didn't see that SGN should accept any blame whatsoever. But we were to discover that it's his way - not accepting blame for anything. We requested that his right hand man, Johnny come into the meeting because a lot of what was being discussed had to do with him. He didn't know what he was doing and we were the recipients of his ineptitude. He defended himself by saying that there were difficulties in getting the camera out to us. We knew that. He also said that the tapes he received (Oh, so he *did* receive them) were blank. Jane finally came into the meeting. We asked for the tapes and camera, stuck the tapes in and proceeded to show them the footage. Joe was dumbfounded and to cover his own embarrassment and ignorance, yelled at Johnny. After that scene, there was a lot of double talk, for which Joe was proficient.

After a few minutes more of "who did what," Joe called his lawyer into the meeting and we discussed the contract between Amazon Films and SGN. Now a lot of lawyer double-talk.

I asked Joe again and again if he wanted to go forward and he assured us that yes, he did. But he told us that money was tight and we would have to hold on. Hold on to what? He still owed us over twenty-five thousand dollars. Jane quietly got up from the table and returned with two checks for five thousand dollars each, which she placed in front of us. We felt a little relieved, but I still had an ache in my stomach about the rest that he owed us. Were we back on track? I hoped so.

The next week we went back to Palm Springs to cover a charity event with Sonny Bono's widow, Congresswoman Mary Bono. We got a great interview with her that we never saw again. This was a recurring problem with SGN. We would do our part, but SGN never followed through in doing their part.

BRENDAN

Then one day I got a telephone call that changed everything. Fran Capra, a previous SGN writer called us from New York and gave us information that floored us. Joe Anthony Lanza was a felon. He had just gotten out of prison the year before on a gas and oil scam with a publicly traded company.

Fran informed us that it was actually her and her writing partner who created "The Estrogen Files." (Not Jane, as Jane implied to us.) And furthermore, they had not been paid for their work. And there were a whole lot of other people behind her waiting for their money from Joe and Jane. Oh, boy. Now we were fried. We knew that we would never get our money if we confronted Joe, but we didn't want to spend one more minute doing anything for SGN.

Fran asked us to be part of a collection agency's attempt to collect money from SGN. We had to think about it for a

196

couple of weeks. During that time, we stayed closely in touch with SGN and didn't pressure them to give us our money. We did politely ask a couple of times though. Even after giving them our expense receipts from Cannes, their accountant, Annie again requested our receipts. We weren't sure if they were losing them or simply throwing them away. We *were* smart enough to give her copies, holding on to the originals. No money came our way. All we got was the runaround. Then we couldn't get through to anyone "important" at SGN. Our phone calls were never returned.

I had been checking on Original Media through the stock market and on Internet company Raging Bull's message board. I discovered that there were a lot of accusations and occasionally, Amazon Films was mentioned. Usually not in a favorable way. I recognized one of the touters as our incompetent, Johnny. Of course, he was disguised as simply an investor who believed in Original Media and SGN. Jane was portrayed sometimes as a scam artist and sometimes as a saint. It was an amusing period - to see the different perspectives of those who knew little of the actual truth. Every once in a while Jane would get on the board and defend herself and SGN. It felt like a circus and became truly comical.

After about a month of not having our calls returned, I went on the board at Raging Bull and sent a message which stated that the relationship between Amazon Films and SGN had ended. Ten minutes later we got a call from Joe. What were we doing? What we were doing was calling it quits. Going public has some advantages.

What was funny was that we were made out to be the bad guys. Joe accused us of being demanding and said that we had spent over fifty thousand dollars of SGN's money at Cannes. I wish. There was a buzz on Raging Bull about Amazon Films for the next two days, then we became old news.

We called Fran and agreed that we would be part of the collection process. She was angry at the Lanzas, and went to great lengths to stop Joe and Jane from taking advantage of anyone else. It's truly laughable how easily crooks can get away with stuff.

Fran went to the SEC (Security and Exchange Commission) about what was going on, but OM was probably at the end of a long list of publicly traded companies being investigated.

We heard from an insider at SGN that Sarah and I were considered troublemakers and were looked upon as disgruntled employees. It was interesting that there were more than a few employees of SGN who thought Sarah and I were cold hearted and petty bitches. Until the time came when those employees didn't get the money that they were owed and then they came over to the "enlightened" side. One of them was Jane's personal vice president. She seemed like an ok person. We just thought she was blinded by the bling too. She couldn't believe that we, or anyone else, thought that Jane and Joe were crooks. Her time came. We heard that they screwed her too. It was hard to listen to a few of those diehards who feverously defended Joe and Jane and then talked trash about the two just like everyone else.

SARAH

As the crazy days unfolded, we were searching for some amount of truth and consolation. Then Fran called one day with the name of Joe's parole officer in Colorado. I called him and told him about the misrepresentations and he said that there wasn't much he could do. He took down the information, but that was it.

BRENDAN

Sarah and I still persisted in asking for the money they owed us, but in our hearts we knew that it was a lost cause. Then one day their "new" lawyer called and we discussed taking stock in the company in exchange for the money SGN owed us. We figured it was better than nothing, so we agreed to 100,000 shares of OM for each of us. Maybe the price would go up. After a few conversations with the attorney over the next two months, he informed us that he could give us our shares of stock - fifty thousand each. At the time, the stock traded at .004 cents. That meant that the fifteen thousand dollars we were owed was worth two hundred dollars to each of us. I told the attorney to stick the stock up his ass. He was offended that we didn't want to take the deal. It was bad enough that the stock was so low, but to cheat us out of 100,000 shares was more than I could handle. It was all so insulting.

I followed Original Media on Raging Bull for a few months, but I lost interest when their stock stared trading at .001 cents. I actually had bought some OM when we first started doing business with SGN. I still have some. I think.

SARAH

Our dealings with Jane and Joe had all happened so fast. We met them in Santa Monica, and a few days later we were being offered a "deal." We didn't do any background checking on Joe and Jane. They were charming and had nice offices and appeared to have lots of money, so why would we think to question anything. We were simply so blinded by the glitter and dangling diamonds, we forgot about due diligence.

Note: LOOK BEFORE YOU LEAP -

GOOGLE TO YOUR HEART'S CONTENT

15

BACK TO THE FUTURE. 1985.

Directed by Robert Zemeckis.

Starring Michael J. Fox and Christopher Lloyd.

Tagline: "Marty McFly's having the time of his life.

The only question is – what time is it?"

SARAH

I had enough. I didn't like this business like Brendan did. I thought that there was more to life. And a lot of the people we dealt with were so slimy, that I couldn't take it anymore. So I sold everything and took off for Italy. Enough. Enough. Enough.

In Italy I lost myself in the beauty, the art and the food. I got a job with the United Nations Food and Agricultural Organization (FAO) and became the Communications

Coordinator of the project, "International Year of the Rice."

FAO was the key UN organization whose main goal was to

feed the world through educating local people in impoverished

countries about their farms, crops and animals. I felt like I was

finally doing something important.

It was a wonderful time. I learned the language and traveled

all over Italy. I even had a side business of arranging mini

tours for American travelers. Life was good. There were

people I met in Italy who wanted to do film projects, but it was

the same thing – no one had money. And the flakes I met there

who said they did – well, it was no different from LA.

16

GLENGARRY GLEN ROSS. 1992.

Directed by James Foley.

Starring Jack Lemmon, Al Pacino and Ed Harris.

Tagline: "Lie. Cheat. Steal. All in a day's work."

Brendan

I also needed a break from the madness of what we had been trying to do for two years, but I needed to make a living. We had spent our own money for two years and now it was gone. And the stock market had fallen apart.

I took a job with a production company, GAT Entertainment which produced family films. I was hired to raise money for them. This was my chance to see how it was done. Boy, did I learn a lot in a few months. They had it mastered. CEO's, owners of businesses and anyone who made over $250,000 annually were called on the telephone. Their names were acquired through a listing service that provided the leads for GAT. This kind of money-raising is done all the time and is called a private placement. It is regulated by the Securities and Exchange Commission and is generally successful when venture capital is plentiful. However, one of the stipulations is that you cannot solicit. You must have an existing relationship with the person who invests. Telemarketing investors is against the regulations. That's exactly what GAT did. As far as I know, they are still doing it. So much for the SEC being on top of stuff.

I saw how easily the money came in and my wheels started turning. I contacted a couple of producers, Jess Mancilla and Henry Charr with whom I had worked in the past and we discussed raising money this way. They had produced over 20 movies, but another production company, PM Entertainment (now defunct) had put the money up for the films. When PM went out of business, they left with the big bucks and Jess and Henry were left with a couple of old movies that weren't going to produce much more money. Jess once said something pretty funny to me. One day he and Henry were invited to the home of one of the partners at PM. As the two of them walked around the mansion, Jess commented that he and Henry bought the master bedroom.

They knew how to produce movies on low low budgets, so I thought this would be a perfect arrangement. I wanted to be involved in the creative process of movie making, but to begin with, I would get the money division going - and create a lucrative and decent place to work. They weren't easily convinced that this was the way to raise money.

I continued to work at GAT, but I was anxious to move on. I couldn't shake the uneasy feeling I had in their callous environment of money making to produce family films. It seemed askew somehow.

One day when we all showed up at the office, no one was there except the lawyer. He called each of us into his office and informed us that there was an internal investigation happening, and no more money could be raised until issues were resolved. That was vague enough. I knew that something was coming down the week before when the accountant quit. When accountants suddenly go, there's something happening – and usually it's not good.

Note: MAKE FRIENDS WITH THE ACCOUNTANT.

(THEN YOU'LL KNOW WHEN THERE'S MONEY TROUBLE)

Even though GAT closed its doors for a few days, I was told that they are still in business making their phone calls and making big bucks. I had to ask myself if I was made of the material that was necessary for this crazy unpredictable business.

As far as I know, Jess and Henry are still making movies too, and I believe that they are doing it their way and reaping the benefits – I hope so.

Too much madness. I took a break – sold my house and left LA. The thought of working in the movie business again made me cringe. I spent the next few months living in NYC and then took off for Italy to write this book with Sarah.

Even though I got calls regularly about projects in LA, I couldn't imagine going back. I had enough too.

After a little thought about where my next adventure would lead me, I bought a house on ten acres outside of Santa Fe, New Mexico. The house is totally solar, I'm basically self-sustained and I love it here. The sky is blue, the air is fresh and the stars shine brightly in the beautiful night sky. I have five dogs that follow me into the mountains on my hikes and fresh vegetables from my garden.

I thought that I had kissed the movie business goodbye when I moved to New Mexico. I had no idea that there was a growing film business and lots of work. But low and behold, there is, and I'm back into it. My first project was a Lions Gate TV pilot that closed shop here after two weeks and moved to Palm Springs. Ah, Show Biz…

SARAH

I don't miss it at all. Well, maybe a little. Brendan and I are already working on our next project.

Sarah Reid returned from Italy, married the man of her dreams and lives in Houston, Texas where she is hoping to be an astronaut for NASA.

Brendan Shepherd currently lives outside of Santa Fe, New Mexico in an off-the-grid house where she's raising rattlesnakes.

Notes to Self

Made in the USA
Las Vegas, NV
09 March 2021